D0770682

DEAL ME IN !
The Use of Playing Cards in Learning and Teaching

by Margie Golick, Ph.D.
Chief Psychologist
Learning Centre
McGill-Montreal Children's Hospital

JEFFREY NORTON PUBLISHERS, INC.
96 Broad Street, Guilford, CT 06437

2nd Edition 1988

Library of Congress Catalog Card Number 73-14124
International Standard Book Number 0-88432 253-X

Copyright © 1973, 1981, 1988 by Margie Golick

All rights reserved. Printed in the United States
of America. No part of this publication may be
reproduced, stored in a retrieval system, or
transmitted, in any form or by any means, electronic,
mechanical, photocopying, recording, or otherwise,
without the prior written permission of the publisher.

To Jody, Jill and Danny—
Shut Up and Deal!

ACKNOWLEDGMENTS

I am especially grateful to my colleagues at the McGill-Montreal Children's Hospital Learning Centre for making me their official card game consultant and for their support and approval of this undertaking.

Some of the initial inspiration for a book about cards came from the children who spent hours every summer in my living-room playing cards with my own children. To Hester, Joel, Michael, David, Ted, Josh, Jed, Nina, Nadine, Paula, Adam, Peter and the Earl of Coventry I say thank you.

This book was really a family project. My children, Jody, Jill and Danny, had an enormous part in every stage of it, and it is as much their book as it is mine. My husband, Peter, learned to live with the sound of the riffle shuffle while the rest of us tried out innumerable versions of games and solitaires and card tricks. Though Peter never played a hand, he consistently helped me turn psychological jargon into English.

Mrs. Frances Foster and the staff and students of St. George's Elementary School, and Miss Peggy Steele and the staff and students of Herbert Symonds School let me come and play cards and take pictures in their classrooms. I deeply appreciate their assistance. Photographs also were taken at the Hamilton-Madison House Child Care Center in New York through the courtesy of Ms. Effie Lui, Director; Association of Black Social Workers through the courtesy of Mrs. Spencer. I appreciate their cooperation.

Above all I want to acknowledge the contribution of hundreds of children with learning disabilities—many now successful adults—who, though they came to me for help, taught me most of what I have come to know about learning and teaching.

CONTENTS

PREFACE TO THE SECOND EDITION

When *Deal Me In!* was first published, my objective was to remind parents and teachers of dozens of card games and card tricks that could be played for educational benefit. The guidelines to their use had grown out of my work with children and adolescents who had disabilities that made some aspects of learning hard for them.

The field of learning disabilities has broadened and deepened in the last 15 years. There are new insights into the underlying neurological differences some of these children have, new emphases in research, new approaches to assessment and remedial teaching. But the practical issues are still the same. We must find out each child's particular talents and specific deficits. We need to let those strengths and weaknesses determine the methods of teaching. We have to find the gaps in their knowledge and try to plug them. We have to determine the skills they need to master and find ways of helping them do so. Above all, we have to make sure the child has a satisfactory social and recreational life and prevent the disability from becoming the major focus of the family's activities.

A deck of cards is still, for me, a valuable tool in achieving these aims. I use it for assessment, for teaching, and to help children and their parents find pleasurable ways to work on reading, spelling, math, memory, and social skills.

When I wrote the book I had directed it to parents of children with learning disabilities and to special-education teachers. I had not anticipated the enthusiasm of teachers and parents in general. I have been delighted by their response. Many liked the idea that old-fashioned play might help their children develop important cognitive and academic skills. Others simply wanted to play, but needed to know rules to games they had forgotten or wanted to learn.

In this edition, I have updated the references for would-be card collectors. I would like to add a useful tip for magicians who perform the "Spelling the Cards" trick on Page 172. It is a mnemonic (memory aid), taught to me by a child, for remembering the pre-arranged order of the cards, 3, 8, 7, Ace, Queen, 6, 4, 2, Jack, King, 10, 9, 5.

"In the year **387** there was **A QUEEN** who was **64**. She had **2** brothers, a **JACK** and a **KING**. One was **10** and the other was **95**."

In the last 15 years I have played cards with children in many parts of the world, played in schools for the deaf and the physically handicapped, and added to my card collection. In the process I learned many new games and card tricks — 100 or so of which I described in *Reading, Writing, and Rummy*. The classic ones described here are still my standbys.

PREFACE

Long before I was consciously aware of their educational side effects, cards had a magical appeal for me. Like a crossword puzzle, a detective story, a tea party and a séance all rolled into one, cards had brought to my own childhood, suspense, sociability, and a bit of the occult.

My earliest relationships, in the small town where I lived, revolved around card games—*Casino* with my grandmother, *Pinochle* with my grandfather, *Whist*, *Rummy*, and *Cribbage* with friends, and hours and hours of *Solitaire*, card tricks, and foretelling the future.

My fascination with cards has not diminished. Although I never play cards with adults, I collect cards, read about them and have been trading card games with children for years.

Even this generation of children which has television to help them pass the time is not immune to the fascinating appeal of playing cards. I was not surprised to see each of my own children pull out a deck whenever there were enough people around for a hand of *Spit* or *Hearts* or whatever their current passion was. After all, cards have been around for more than five hundred years, and their forerunners probably go back thousands of years. With such an impressive history, it seems likely that the games that have evolved over the centuries will continue to fascinate and entertain for centuries to come.

It seemed natural to me as a psychologist working with children to add card games to my bag of tricks and to bring them out to help youngsters relax—as a way of getting to know them better and of seeing how they go about learning something new. Children who came to see me, in turn, taught me dozens of games and tricks that were new to me.

As my collection grew and my experience at playing cards with children increased, I realized what a tremendous teaching tool I had. Now after more than twenty years of "deal-

1

ing" with children, I am convinced that a deck of cards is an invaluable piece of equipment for the psychologist, teacher, or parent who wants to make sure that a child will develop and practice some of the skills he will need at school.

Over the years I have managed to turn many of my colleagues into card sharks. In educational workshops that looked like gambling casinos, I have shared my ideas and my collection of games with hundreds of parents and teachers, teachers of regular classes, teachers of children with learning disabilities, and teachers of children with physical or mental or emotional handicaps. Their enthusiasm for card games as a teaching aid encouraged me to compile in writing the games, their educational rationale, and some of the pointers I have picked up from the children who played with me.

INTRODUCTION

As a psychologist in a center for children who have trouble learning at school, I have spent more than twenty years pondering the paradoxes in children's learning ability. I have studied and taught highly intelligent children of school age—some of them gifted in mathematics—who found it overwhelmingly difficult to learn to read; and I have watched many four-year olds teach themselves to read with no apparent effort. I have seen youngsters who could read and write, and express themselves with great skill, but who, even at age ten or eleven, could not do a simple arithmetical computation, say, 1 + 2, without counting on their fingers.

3

Over the years, I have charted the profiles of abilities and disabilities of thousands of children and visited classrooms for normal children and for all kinds of special children. I have watched some children lap up information and others fail to learn in spite of the good teachers who were trying to teach them.

Always I have been preoccupied with specifying what children need to know to become successful learners in school. Some of their needs are obvious.

1. They have to know how to sit still for a little while and look; they have to know how to sit still and listen.

2. They have to develop the ability to make fast and accurate visual judgments. In order to learn arithmetic (or even to cross the street), a child has to be a good estimator of distance, direction, and number in the three dimensional world. In the two-dimensional world of print, he has to be able to recognize very small differences in the shape, size, and position of tiny little squiggles on a page.

3. Children have to know their native language. In order to learn in a classroom, they have to be able to follow directions and explanations that are given at a normal speed and in a normal tone of voice. They have to learn to hear barely perceptible contrasts between words and between phrases that differ in only one sound or in the stress patterns found in ordinary conversation.

4. They have to be able to talk about what they see, hear, and feel; they have to translate ideas and experiences into words so that they can share them and the teacher can find out what they know and what they need to know; children use words to help them remember what they have learned. Learning a language means learning not just the words that label things, actions, and qualities but the complex rules our language has evolved for putting words together to convey an infinite number of ideas.

5. Children have to be able to move with precision—arms and legs, eyes and hands. The importance of good coordination for a satisfying social and recreational life is obvious. But even sedentary activities like reading and writing demand great control and flexibility of the muscles involved in moving the eyes, hands, and fingers.

6. An efficient learner does not take in information passively, store it, and spit it out again. He develops strategies for remembering, categorizing, reorganizing, and retrieving. He tries to make sense of things, to see relationships, and to discover causes and effects; and when new facts he meets are not in accord with his theories, he learns to revise the theories and develop new plans of attack. This active searching for regularities, for order, and for meaning goes on from infancy to adulthood.

7. Probably most important of all to learning at school is a child's general well-being. A good learner, like a good boy scout, is not just prepared. He's cheerful. Even if he does not enjoy every minute of the learning process (as he exper-

iences it in the classroom), he has a mental storehouse of past pleasures he can fall back on or look forward to when he is overwhelmed by some of the inevitable drudgery of the school day. Because he has had plenty of joyous, satisfying learning experiences and has a sense of his own powers for acquiring new skills, he is not likely to get depressed too easily when the going gets rough. If he is discouraged by a temporary failure, he can be cheered by the memory of many successes.

8. Many of the pleasures of learning and living come from relationships with other people. A child will be receptive to the teacher's teachings only if he has learned to care about the adults in his world. This kind of caring grows out of his own experiences of being cared about and respected and enjoyed. If past experience has taught him to like grown-ups, he might even be able to make allowances now and then for the unreasonable behavior of a crabby teacher.

9. Still, survival in the classroom takes more than good relationships with adults. A child has to know how to work

and play with children. He has to be part of their culture, know the informal code that guides behavior, know rules of games, the catchwords, slogans, routines, rituals, and passions that permeate that world.

How do children learn all these things? Nobody *really* knows. The thousands of studies about learning that have been conducted on rats and pigeons and college sophomores have taught us many things about the learning process but very little about how most children manage to know all the things they know when they get to school. So much seems to happen so fast that all we can do is guess. Some theorists believe that human beings must be biologically programmed to learn the things they acquire with such amazing speed.

The human nervous system, they maintain, is uniquely predisposed to make the sensory discriminations, to notice the regularities, patterns, and relationships that life demands.

Other theorists attribute the child's amazing progress to the unusual teaching ability of human mothers and fathers. Without any special training for the job most parents manage to transmit their language, values, customs, and even their fears and anxieties to their offspring.

7

One thing is certain: children take an *active* part in the learning process. They *practice* the skills they are in the process of mastering. This seems to be an important function of *play*. The constant throwing of spoons over the sides of highchairs, the opening and closing of cupboard doors, the taking apart and putting together of coffee pots, the endless treks up and down stairs all effectively help to develop motor skills. Before he can talk a baby babbles, apparently for the fun of it, perhaps getting his speech apparatus in training. Later on, alone in his crib, he actively drills himself on the sound combinations and sentence patterns of his language. The preschool role-playing games of "house," "school," and "space man" help children figure out the adult world, provide rehearsal for the real thing, allow for give and take relationships, and offer children the chance to develop their resourcefulness and inventiveness.

Through their own efforts and some external guidance, most children arrive at school well-equipped for the years ahead.

For reasons that are not well understood, there are intelligent children—perhaps ten to fifteen percent of all children —who need more time and extra help to acquire the perceptual, motor, verbal, intellectual, and social skills school demands. Such children are said by professionals to have "learning disabilities," a descriptive cover term for the difficulties they have in learning some kinds of things. For children with learning disabilities to succeed at school, we have to find ways to make explicit the regularities and relationships other children have discovered for themselves. This may mean breaking down a complex task into simpler parts so the child can master it step by step. It may mean that a child needs longer exposure to the material to be learned, frequent repetitions, or more extensive practice of an emerging skill.

Not surprisingly, these same children who take a long time to add a new word or a new fact or an integrated pattern of movements to their repertoire are often the very ones who balk at boring drill and who are quick to tire of repetitive tasks.

The challenge in helping these youngsters is to find activities that are inherently interesting, that will motivate them to work at something over and over again just because it is so intriguing, so challenging, or so much fun. Although I do not believe that all hard work should be sugar-coated, I *do* feel that the load for the youngster with a learning disability should be lightened whenever it is possible. If I can find a gimmick or a gadget or a game that will help a child ultimately become more adept at reading, writing, or arithmetic, I will always prefer it to a more conventional approach.

In my search for effective teaching aids, I have studied and used dozens of different kinds of commercially-made educational programs, remedial techniques, and teaching materials, I have conferred with the originators of some of the best of these. I have even participated in the creation of special materials designed to make children more efficient learners. But even with the proliferation of carefully programmed books and games, expensive educational toys, science kits, aids to the new math and preschcol readiness equipment, if I could choose only one teaching aid besides pencil and paper, it would be an ordinary deck of playing cards. In those fifty-two pieces of pasteboard are limitless possibilities for developing manual dexterity, visual efficiency, concepts of space, time and number, principles of sorting and grouping, and the forethought, logic, planning ability, and mental alertness needed to handle many intellectual tasks.

More than any other "educational toy" I know of, a deck of cards has the potential to exploit the child's readiness, through play, to take an active role in the learning process.

GUIDELINES FOR USE

I have tried to incorporate, in the sections that follow, all the comments, criticisms and answers to questions that emerged in discussion with parents and teachers. Although parents and teachers share the task of educating children and helping them to become competent, resourceful people, because of their very different situations, the full-time guardians and the part-time guardians have different sets of concerns. It would seem appropriate to give a few guidelines for these different groups.

ASIDE TO THE CLASSROOM TEACHER

I would like to see several decks of cards in every classroom in the country. They will have many uses in an ordinary day. From kindergarten through high school, the privilege of playing a hand or two can be extended to children who finish their work early; an appropriate game can be the

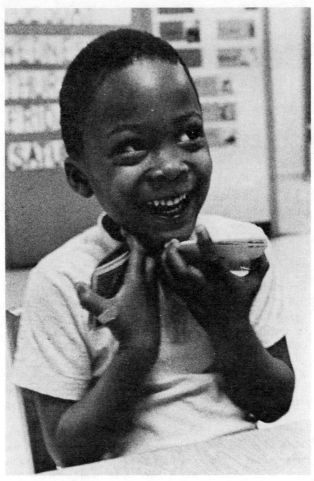

math activity of the day for some of the children. In foreign language classes, the children's oral participation in French, Spanish, or whatever is easily elicited if they are playing a familiar game. If the teacher feels it necessary to teach to children who speak a nonstandard dialect some standard forms of English, these can be practiced in the guise of a well-chosen card game. One teacher I know who runs her class on behavior modification principles, uses her stock of card tricks as the ultimate reward for desirable behavior. The children in her class earn points for speedy and accurate work. When a child has accumulated enough points he can trade them in for the secret of one of the teacher's tricks. I have seen another skilful teacher launch a shy child into "public speaking", by getting him to perform a card trick, with suitable patter, for the class.

TO THE TEACHER OF A "SPECIAL" CLASS

I have talked to many teachers who work exclusively with children who have learning problems or who teach children with more severe handicaps. They find it rewarding to be able to teach in small groups and help these children overcome or learn to circumvent their very real problems.

But all of them deplore the isolation of the children in their charge from the "normal" child and from "normal" activities. Apart from its value as a remedial tool, a deck of cards can help to break down barriers. The disabled child especially needs to learn games that will allow him to play with other children; many card games demand little in the way of physical or linguistic skills. The blind child will need Braille cards. Children with cerebral palsy may need a special holder for their cards. It might take deaf children longer to learn the rules, but they will need no concessions in the play. Even the so-called hyperactive child, highly distractible and disorganized in his approach to "work" has been known to play games by the hour with no noticeable lapse in attention. If the teacher wants to help her children integrate, she can teach them some card games, invite a small group of regular class children in for a card party, and let the children discover for themselves that they can have fun together.

TO PARENTS

Often, after I have assessed a child who is having trouble at school, it seems appropriate to involve him in activities that will help him develop some of the skills he lacks. Because of the scarcity of specialists, the parents sometimes have to double as remedial teachers; and even when one of the special teachers is available for weekly or twice-a-week sessions, it is the parents who have to see that assignments are done on a regular basis, and keep interest and enthusiasm high. That's when knowing some card games with educational fringe benefits comes in handy. Families that already play cards together need no advice from me.

My card-playing lore has been helpful to parents who had forgotten all the card games they ever knew, or who thought that teaching card games to the children would be a waste of valuable time. I have taught—or more often, have sent my teenage daughter, Jill, to teach—mother and father and all the children in a family some good games that would be of particular help to one of the children.

But I always give parents who embark on a course of constructive card playing a word of warning. An incident that stands out in my memory will help me make my point. Long ago, I watched friends of mine present their five-year-old son with a new toy "especially designed by educators" for preschoolers to help them improve their eye-hand coordination, form perception, and attention span. The little boy was delighted with it. He carried the blocks around, ran his toy trucks over them, piled them and threw them up in the air. Then his parents sat down with him and tried over and over again to impress upon him how the parts were "supposed" to be used. I'll never forget the bewildered expression on his face as he looked up at them and asked, "Isn't this a *toy*?"

Parents have to remember in their educational zeal that card games are *games*. They will be effective as teaching aids only as long as they are fun and as long as parents and children enjoy playing them together. It is often painful or boring for a parent to have to supervise written homework, or to "hear" spelling, or to try to explain English grammar. Even those of us who are highly effective at teaching other people's children, often lose our objectivity and our cool when we try to teach our own child something as crucial to his future as multiplication or French verbs.

But teaching and playing a game is another matter altogether. We are investing time in something that can bring hours of pleasurable interaction. Even in the likely eventuality that *our* attention span for games will be shorter than the kids', none of us is so devoid of gambling spirit that the possibility of winning does not enhance the activity. And when the opponent is one's own offspring, our defeats too, provide a vicarious satisfaction.

TO THE SCHOOL PSYCHOLOGIST AND REMEDIAL TEACHER

If part of your job is to assess a child's abilities, you are concerned with getting to know many sides of the real individual, not just the over-controlled, anxious, or even belligerent side of him that a visit to a psychologist's office might bring out. That is why—for the first little while—I forget about the Wechsler and the Stanford-Binet and all the contrived "games" we ask children to play with us, and pull out an honest-to-goodness deck of cards. "Do you know any card games?" I might ask. It is hard for the most

15

guarded youngster not to loosen up and start to enjoy himself as we exchange games, play a few hands, and argue over who took in the last trick. After twenty minutes or so, I have as much information about the children I see as I might get from several hours spent administering, scoring, and interpreting a battery of standardized psychological tests. I certainly learn something about their finger dexterity, handedness, visual efficiency, attention span, and mental alertness. If they have tried to teach me games or card tricks I learn a fair amount about their language, and about their ability to organize and communicate ideas. If I have tried to teach him a game, I have pretty good insight into how he learns most effectively.

I will have had a chance to see whether he can learn from verbal explanations alone. If he has difficulty, I can find out whether it is helpful to him to simplify my language, repeat the instructions, slow them up, add nonverbal demonstrations, or cut down on outside distractions. Then, if the card session is followed up with psychological tests, the tests can be used, not just routinely, or as a massive battery, but to answer specific questions and to check hypotheses that have been raised by the informal contact.

SKILLS THAT CARD GAMES CAN HELP DEVELOP

Although the skills that underlie successful learning are highly interrelated, it can be useful to delineate (albeit somewhat artificially) some of the advantages of card games as a teaching and learning tool.

MOTOR SKILLS

A problem common to many children in the first years of school, and particularly children with learning disabilities, is poor handwriting. Their work is set down slowly, is messy or illegible, and consistently deplored by teachers. Many of these youngsters hold the pencil awkwardly in a tight, inflexible grip, dislike writing and avoid it whenever they can. They shy away, too, from activities that call for any manual skills, such as drawing, painting, carpentry, and crafts. Nevertheless, in order to handle a pencil well, a child has to learn to use his hands and fingers competently. He has to be able to differentiate between the two hands, to develop preference for and greater competence in one, and still employ the other as an assistant. He has to learn to use his fingers separately and together and especially learn to use thumb and forefinger as partners. Handling, shuffling, dealing a deck, picking up the cards, learning to fan a "hand" of cards all offer practice in an extensive range of hand and finger movements.

RHYTHM

Closely related to the motor difficulties of some children with learning disabilities is their dim awareness or understanding of rhythm. They show little appreciation of the orderly timing that is needed in physical activities, that underlies easy speech and the effortless understanding of another speaker, and that is essential to the appreciation of music and poetry. Playing cards exposes children to a variety of simple rhythms and gives them practice in maintaining them.

An efficient dealer hands out his cards in a steady rhythm. The auditory pattern varies according to the number of players: 1.- 2 - 3; 1 - 2 - 3; 1 - 2 - 3 - 4; 1 - 2 - 3 - 4. A child can learn to *hear* these rhythms. Have him close his eyes and try to tell by listening how many players there are.

As a budding dealer gradually develops the art and hands the cards to one player after another, he gets the added motor rhythm. Muscular sensations from the steady, often-repeated movements are added to the visual and auditory sensations; and with the hours of practice that addiction to playing cards inevitably brings, these rhythms will become almost second nature to the child.

There are also visual rhythms or patterns that card games help to introduce. Alternation, for example, is a principle that must be followed in some games when red cards are placed on black, and black on red. A number of games require one card faced down, one card faced up in turn.

There are several solitaires that have unique layouts, with an implicit rhythm or pattern.

SEQUENCE

There are some children who not only have problems with rhythm, but even more troublesome difficulties in understanding arrangements in space and time. They seem unable to grasp the *order* in time of a series of sounds, or movements, or activities. Ideas of first, second, third confuse them because they fail to sort out the relative position of each member of a series of successive parts. Similarly, they fail to learn spatial arrangements which have a predetermined sequence—from left to right or from top to bottom. This, too, seems to be because they have not learned to take the order of elements into account in their perception of a configuration. They may note the color, size, shape, and number of parts, but not their relative positions.

Card games provide innumerable opportunities to learn about, to appreciate the need for, to practice, and to "feel in one's bones," every kind of sequencing. The deal follows a prescribed order. Every game means taking turns, and repeatedly watching the sequence of plays until one's turn comes around again. Younger children, or children who have special difficulty in this area, will inevitably play out of turn. The noisy response of the group will help them learn the lesson, which for a while may have to be relearned each time they get into a game with a different number of players.

Then there are all the opportunities in the games themselves for learning about numerical sequence. Games like *Stop and Go*, and *I Doubt It*, require each player in turn to play a card that is just one higher; for example, a three on a two or a four after a three. There are the runs of *Rummy*—4, 5, 6 in the same suit; the straights of *Poker*—7, 8, 9, 10, Jack; and there are the up and down sequences of *Fan Tan*, *Solitaire*, and related games.

A SENSE OF DIRECTION

A poorly developed sense of direction seems to underlie the difficulties some children have in learning to read and write. It impairs their ability to discriminate letters that differ only in orientation (e.g., b and d, p and q); it leads to confusion in knowing where to start to attack a line of printed words or a single word; it may lead to mirror writing; it can contribute to poor arithmetic skills when a child forgets which side he begins with in adding or subtracting with two digit numbers. The lack of a clear-cut sense of left and right is certainly a handicap in most sports.

In card games, too, direction is important. Cards are dealt clockwise to the players, that is, to the dealer's left. Deal passes to the *left*. Playing turns pass to the left. *Solitaire* layouts and *Spit* layouts are from left to right. An efficient dealer must become aware of the difference in skill between the two hands.

Long sessions at the card table help children learn the importance of taking direction into consideration. The repetition helps to build in an awareness of the difference between right and left. This, in turn, helps to reinforce the left to right movement that is essential to reading and writing.

VISUAL SKILLS

Even the easiest card games demand visual discrimination. There are games demanding only color discrimination. These are good games for youngsters who do not yet know suit and number. Games in which the suits must be kept apart give practice in form discrimination. Many children learn to recognize numbers through some of the simple matching games. At first, it may only be the pattern of spots that is discriminated, later, the numbers themselves.

Learning to tell some numbers apart, say, a 2 from a 5 or a 9 from a 6, will be aided by the spots (the suit markings) which can be counted or perceived as a pattern. The novice may at first have to look carefully to tell the face cards apart. I know preschoolers who learned their first letters and the sounds to attach to them from the J, Q, K, and A on playing cards.

But, the discriminations of color, shape, and number are only preliminaries. Nearly all card games call for constant

21

visual alertness. In cards, as in reading, a motor or verbal response is often triggered by a visual cue. In *Slap Jack*, *Snap*, *Bow to the King*, and *Spit* the players strive for speed and accuracy of visual recognition and response.

Visual tracking (the ability to move the eyes smoothly and efficiently to scan any plane and spot important details) is practiced on a vertical plane every time a player inspects his fan-shaped hand to select a card—as in *Fish*, *Earl of Coventry*, and *Hearts*, and dozens of other games; and on a horizontal plane every time he plays a game of *Solitaire* or inspects a layout on the table. Equally valuable is the rapid shifting of gaze from table to hand and back again required by some games; this provides an opportunity to practice a skill needed by a child in class who has to sit at his desk and copy from the blackboard.

Concentration is the game that makes a good visual memory worth while. The cards and their positions must be remembered in this game of skill which children are often better at than adults. This seems to be a great game for strengthening the inefficient visual recall of most poor spellers.

NUMBER CONCEPTS

The easiest way I know to teach a four-, five- or six-year old to recognize the numbers and the pattern of spots associated with each, is to introduce him to the game of *Go Fish*. I worked with one six-year old who had spent a year in kindergarten, and half a year in first grade without being able to remember which number was which. His distractibility, his clumsiness, and his spatial confusion contributed to his difficulties in the classroom. Yet, after I had taught him the game, he mastered instant recognition of the numbers from 1 to 10 in a week of playing *Go Fish* with his mother.

"Do you have any sixes?" she would say, at first holding up the card for him to see. After comparing it with each card in his hand, he would hand her a matching one, or say, "Go Fish." Then, he would pick a card out of his hand, hold it up and ask, "Do you have any of these?" and she would say, "Any threes?—Let me see, yes, here's a three." Playing the game, which he loved, brought repeated exposure to the numerals and the number of spots they stood for, always paired with the number names supplied by his mother. Before very long, he was using the numbers correctly himself.

However, card games teach more about numbers than their names. The players are continously exposed to a wide range of properties of many numbers. Suppose he is involved with three other players in a game. Consider all the ways he learns "four-ness." He *sees* the players; the rhythm of the deal has a unique auditory pattern; when he is the dealer, he *feels* the four separate movements towards the players as he hands around the cards; the cards are dealt out evenly; when four are playing (instead of two or three) the deal takes longer; more time elapses for his turn to play, or the deal to come around again.

And, from the cards themselves, he learns the fascinating properties of a deck of 52—4 suits, 13 cards in each, 2 pairs of every denomination. With two and four players, the cards can be dealt out evenly; with 3, 5 or 6, they cannot. In some games, he must count out a specific number of cards for each deal—6 for *Fish*; 7 for *Kings*; 8 for *Inflation*. Through dealing, he gradually learns (and often from his errors and the uneven hands that result) to make the one-to-one correspondence between objects and number words that is a basis for understanding arithmetic.

Sharing a group of objects among a number of individuals, as a dealer does, is a precursor to understanding division. (Ask any experienced young card player "how many 4's in 52?" and he will answer in a flash "13"; and "how many 5's in 52?"—"10 and 2 left over.") My own children always dazzled their kindergarten teachers with their lightning cal-

culation of "3 into 52." But anyone who has ever played three-handed *Hearts*, where the 2 of diamonds is removed from the deck, and each player gets 17 cards, knows that $52 \div 3 = 17$, remainder 1.

Handing out the cards two at a time; or three at a time (as in *Manille* and other games of the *Euchre* variety), and counting up the pairs after a game of *Fish,* or the quartets after a game of *Authors,* may be a child's first systematic exercise in counting in groups.

Notions of *more* and *less* are developed in most games of cards, where tricks are counted. The ideas of *greater* than, and *smaller* than; *higher* and *lower; more* and *less;* are learned well through games like *War, Beat the Jack Out of the House, Poker, Manille,* and *Hearts.* Moving up and down

25

the number line is rehearsed in *Fan Tan, Solitaire,* and related games.

Adding is practiced in keeping score, in tallying points, especially in games where cards have different values (e.g., *Casino, Manille, Yukon,* and *Rummy*). In *Hearts,* where points are counted against the players, there is an opportunity to subtract points from one's total, and even to get into negative numbers. There are games where adding is part of the playing tactics. *Casino* and *A Hundred and One* (where children play with number combinations up to 13 and 14), *Black Jack* (where there is a chance to learn every conceivable combination of numbers that can total 21), *Macao* (where the players strive to have their cards total 9), betting games, and games played with counters or chips multiply the possibilities for arithmetical practice.

There are a number of card tricks, and at least one Solitaire that depend on the mathematical properties of the deck. To work some, the child must add mentally; in others, add and subtract, and even multiply in one or two. Budding magicians find the tricks so fascinating that they perform them over and over for their own entertainment, mastering the trick, but at the same time, unconsciously drilling themselves in rapid mental calculation. Putting these tricks in their hands is more effective teaching than dozens of pages of arithmetic homework.

Different card games call for different ways of categorizing the cards—in terms of color, in *Red and Black*; by denomination in *Go Fish* and *Old Maid*; in terms of suit in *Inflation, Hearts,* and *Flashlight*. This leads, if not to the vocabulary of set theory, to notions of sets and subsets. Card games, too, help promote an awareness of chance and probability. Exposed to innumerable shufflings and new deals, the young player begins to recognize that the mixing process is a randomization process, that it is unpredictable, irreversible and leads to an infinite number of possible arrangements. He gets a feeling for "chance" and from this is able to recognize nonchance events. If a cheater has stacked the deck and produces a nonrandom series of events (consistently gets all the Aces, for example), the experienced player can spot the nonrandom causality at work.

Later, a child begins to understand probabilities. If he cannot know for certain what card will turn up next, or what card his partner holds, for example, he can guess. His guesses are determined by his ability to estimate the probabilities. This will be based on his understanding of chance, his knowledge of the structure of the deck, and his memory of what has already happened. If he is playing a betting game, he goes one step further and raises the ante on the basis of his calculation of the odds that his guess is right.

VERBAL SKILLS

Many inefficient learners have little facility with language. They may miss the point of verbal directions, of explanations, and jokes, even in ordinary conversation. They have trouble expressing ideas, describing objects, or narrating events. Sometimes this stems from poor auditory discrimination or a short auditory attention span; sometimes it stems from poor facility for grasping linguistic conventions. The child with poor language may have a restricted vocabulary. He may be vague about words or be unable to figure out, from hearing a word in several situations, the full range of its meaning. His grammar may be faulty. Phrases or arrangements of words and syllables that occur over and over again in the speech of others have not been automatically linked together in his verbal repertoire, so that he can express himself easily without groping for words.

In the simplified world of the card games where the stimuli are reduced, where players are clear about what is being talked about, and the same situations occur over and over again, a large new vocabulary can be introduced and practiced. Some of the new words may have wider application (number names, pairs, turns, odd, even, most, least, etc.). Some may refer only to the cards and games themselves (trick, suit, trump), but the experience of learning a word and being able to use it meaningfully has a stimulating effect on overall vocabulary growth. The practice in listening and correctly discriminating a new word increases the skills demanded in efficient auditory attention and perception.

Some games call for the use of whole phrases, and thus provide the opportunity to practice them repeatedly until they are effortless and automatic, to practice arranging words in the appropriate order, and to use correct grammatical forms. This practice, in turn, facilitates the learning of other phrases.

The *"Fish"* formula, "Do you have any sixes?" practices the question form and the use of the plural.

> "Here's a (King) as good as can be
> Here's another as good as he
> Here's the best of all the three
> And here's the Earl of Coventry."

This rhyme, repeated 13 times in every hand of *Earl of Coventry*, gives the player a feel for rhyme and for rhythm, and it gives him practice in the use of the comparative construction ("as good as") and the superlative ("the best"). "Good morning, Madam," "How do you do, Sir," and "I doubt it," are all intact units of social speech. These and other units of social speech are practiced dozens of times if the appropriate card game is chosen.

INTELLECTUAL SKILLS

Although there is a major element of chance that operates in every card game, players soon discover that in nearly all of them there are strategies to be cultivated and intellectual skills that help to defeat the opponents.

Card games demand attention, concentration, and mental alertness. While playing the games a child who may be distractible in other situations, focuses his attention and sharpens his wit. Inevitably, he is learning to learn.

He is learning, too, of the necessity for order and organization that will stand him in good stead in more academic intellectual tasks. He sees that, for efficient play, cards picked up at the outset of each deal must be arranged in a logical way: in suits, if the game demands it (e.g., *Hearts, Flashlight*), or in terms of denomination, if it is another kind of game (*Fish, Earl of Coventry*). However, as in any intellectual pursuit, his categories cannot be rigidly conceived. In many games, a card must be considered as a member of more than one class, and treated now in one role, then in another. (Consider a 6 of spades in *Rummy* that can be placed beside another 6 in anticipation of three of a kind, then pulled out of that slot to complete the run of spades: 5, 6, 7.) The wider the variety of games played, the greater grows the ability to isolate the attributes of objects and categorize them differentially.

Mental flexibility is a must in cards. The player must be ready to change his set from game to game: where the rules differ, where the object of the game differs (to get all the cards in *War*, to get rid of all your cards first in *Inflation*), to gain key cards in *Casino*, and to avoid key cards in *Hearts*. Within games too, he must be set to respond in a number of different ways. In *Slap Jack*, he must slap *only* the Jack; in *Bow to the King*, he greets each face card differently and slaps the Ace, and in some games, he must be prepared to react differently at different times to the same card. In *Black Jack* and *A Hundred and One*, an Ace is worth either 1 or 11.

Another intellectual asset fostered by playing card games is the ability to keep many factors in mind. In some games, this will include the rank of the cards, or their point value; remembering what cards have been played, and looking ahead to what other players are likely to do.

Just as the clever student works out strategies for problem-solving, the skillful card player develops strategies in every game. It may mean withholding a card lest it give an advantage to an opponent (*Fan-Tan* or *Spit*), or leading a card he has more than one of (*Earl of Coventry*), or getting rid of his high cards (in *Rummy*).

As the game proceeds, play will be determined not only by the cards or conventional strategies, but also by a player's appraisal of the situation. This will range from hunches based on intuition or wishful thinking in younger children (who may believe that if they concentrate hard enough, a sought after card will turn up), to playing the odds when an older child learns to think in probability terms and, knowing what cards are in his hand, what cards have already been played, and the composition of the deck, makes a guess about his opponent's hand and calculates the advisability of a particular play. The socially perceptive child may learn to capitalize on his judgment of other players' facial expressions, or even their "poker faces" to help him divine the cards he cannot see.

Alertness, flexibility, ability to categorize, to consider many variables at once, to think logically, to estimate probabilities are intellectual skills that are essential for mathematics, science, logic, and every kind of academic pursuit. They are developed in card games. And in this kind of activity which is self-perpetuating (because it is fun) and nonauthoritarian (because the skills are acquired through give and take with peers), the less able learn tactics from the more able, and have plenty of chance to perfect them.

SOCIAL SKILLS

For many children who are awkward or easily disorganized in large groups, who never get invited to join in a baseball game, who never play hockey successfully, who are duds on a dance floor, the ability to play a few card games may be the passport to many social groups.

A six-year-old who cannot ride a bike with the other kids in the neighborhood, may get his share of socialization if he can invite a few of them inside for some sedentary games on a rainy afternoon. Eight- and nine-year olds once seduced by cards may, from time to time, spend hours around a card table or on the floor shunning all other activities to the despair of the mothers, who cry "It's such a nice day, why don't you play outside?" For teenagers who cannot make the sports teams, there are always willing opponents for *Cribbage, Whist, Bridge, Poker,* and *Black Jack*.

The chance to be with children of the same age, not just to watch television side by side, but to interact, to engage in partnership and competition with peers, and to be immersed in the culture of childhood with its own jargon, its rules, its obligations, is essential to the business of growing up. The socialization process may bring heated arguments, angry insults, cries of "cheater!", "I did not!", "You did so"; and it may involve many taking sides against one. Sometimes the observer worries about the pressures on a vulnerable youngster; yet children who would crumble if an adult spoke to them harshly, seem able to handle the scorn or reprimands of their playmates and to modify their behavior appropriately.

I saw a good example of this when I was visited at home once by a highly distractible youngster. He had just been expelled from the first-grade classroom because his teacher could not cope with his excessive talk which was usually irrelevant, inappropriate, and disruptive. In order that I might have a chance to talk to his mother, I got my three children to invite him to join their card game. He had no trouble learning the rules, but his incessant questions and long-winded comments were slowing up the game and irritating the other players. Exasperated, one of them finally said, "Will you shut up and deal!", and he did.

It is through this kind of give and take, through criticism and disagreements, that the child becomes less egocentric and better able to see the logic of rules, and the reciprocal gains of co-operation. Ultimately he becomes more objective, rational, and social.

Cards cut across ages and sexes. There are many games suitable to preschoolers and teenagers alike. Players of widely varying abilities can have fun together with *Bango, Lottery, Havana*. Most families can use the fun and excitement that involvement in a game brings to help promote friendly activities and feelings among the siblings.

In many school and neighborhood groups, boys and girls who have played contentedly together up to the ages of eight or nine generally find little common ground for a few years when the girls turn to skipping ropes and dolls, and the boys to competitive sports. If given a chance, they can meet on equal terms over a card game and maintain their ties, so that the inevitable reunion at adolescence is natural and uncontrived.

There are often extra social dividends from partnership games. *Whist* and *Bridge* for older children, *Yukon* for younger ones, or any number of games that can be adapted to team play. Such play brings the experience of co-operating, modifying behavior to suit mutual ends, sharing, communicating, consulting, and putting aside immediate gains for long-range partnership goals.

The partisan feelings engendered by the temporary partnership in a game sometimes go deep enough to create a bond between two children that did not exist before the game began, and that continues when the game is over. I remember one neighborhood group that had a hanger-on, barely tolerated by the others because he was younger and less competent. In a card game where they cut the deck for partners, he drew one of the most popular boys, who accepted him with resignation. Nevertheless, allied against the others in the rivalry of the game, a real tie grew up between the two of them which lasted when they moved on to the next activity. The outsider was actually *chosen* by the older boy for his team in a street game. Once accepted by the leader, his place in the group was assured. A skillful teacher can exploit these fringe benefits of cards by choosing her games strategically, and by helping to structure the teams.

LEARNING TO PLAY

Teachers and parents sometimes ask, "If a child has a learning disability, won't he have as much trouble learning to play games as he has had in learning to read or do arithmetic?" Many children certainly will find it impossible to learn from written instructions which confuse even the teachers now and then. It will be up to the teacher though, to learn the game and find a way to transmit it to the child. An inefficient learner may have trouble catching on unless his teacher uses those techniques she might use in helping him with his schoolwork. If a child has chronic difficulty paying attention, she will want to make sure there are few background distractions. She will see that he is not tired or upset and she will make the periods of instruction no longer than he can tolerate at one sitting. She may have to teach the game first in a one-to-one setting. Many children have difficulty attending to and following directions intended for a group, but have no difficulty with instructions and explanations given directly to them, spoken reasonably slowly in short units. In a face-to-face situation, the child may feel more at ease about asking for repetition or further explanations where necessary.

Games are best taught with demonstrations accompanying words. Children watching a few hands of an unfamiliar game seem to have an uncanny knack for grasping the requirements, the lingo, and even the strategies with very little formal instruction. They certainly get a chance to see how much fun it is. If it is not possible for a novice to watch experienced players play the game, the child should be helped to play the first few rounds with both hands exposed, and all plays explained.

Instruction of a game should never include words the learner has not been taught separately. If he is learning *Rummy* make sure he has already learned what is meant by "a run" or "meld." Even a simple game like *Go Fish* requires the prospective player to know what a "pair" is. Teachers and parents sometimes assume that a child understands a common word that has a slightly different meaning in noncard playing situations. ("Aces are high" means nothing to a child whose only association with the word "high" is "out of reach".) Or they take certain playing card conventions for granted, forgetting that they have to be taught. (I once told a youngster, glibly, that a "pair" was "two-of-a-kind." He spent a frustrating few minutes in a game of *Fish* trying to locate two threes of diamonds before we cleared up the misunderstanding.) It is especially important when there is a learning problem to make sure *each step is understood* because children who are used to missing the point of teachers' explanations, tend to tune out as soon as they become the least bit confused, thereby compounding the confusion. After a game is learned, it is a good idea to reinforce this learning by playing the game several times in succession right away, and again sometime in the next few days, to make sure it sticks.

ABOUT CARDS

The virtues of cards as a teaching tool include their availability, cheapness, and portability. Almost every child has access to a deck. Any kind of deck will do. In the illustrations in this book, I have shown cards with large numerals; and because they are so easy to read, I like to use these when I play with children. Sometimes, to add variety, I introduce an unusual deck. I have a collection of miniature decks of cards especially useful for playing *Solitaire* in cramped quarters. Round cards and "crooked" decks are available at novelty shops. Both seem to me to be a little easier to hold and fan for an inexperienced player whose fingers are still clumsy.

In using cards to develop mathematical notions in young children, there are a number of special decks that come in handy. We want to be sure that a child who can give the denomination of a card knows more than just the name of the numeral. We can make certain that he associates the number name with a quantity (the cardinal value of the number) by playing with a deck that has no numerals—only spots. My deck, bought at Williamsburg, Virginia, is a reproduction of 18th Century cards. Similarly, as a check on a child's ability to associate quantity with the numeral alone, we can play a game like *War* with a deck that prevents him from counting the spots. The Museum of Modern Art in New York sells a contemporary deck with no spots in the middle, only large clear numerals.

For older children, or younger students in the "New Math" who are learning about binary numbers, the Honeywell

Company puts out the kind of deck computers would use if they played cards. Each number is represented in its binary (base 2) form as well as its normal base 10 form.

When cards are lost from decks, as they are in the best of families, save the left-overs. A deck made up of old cards from several decks is fun to play with when children want to exercise their memories and try to keep track of face-down cards by their backs. To get additional practice in memorizing, play *Concentration* with a deck made up of a number of different backs.

For more than three hundred years playing cards have been produced with backs or faces especially designed to instruct, or advertise or commemorate. There are cards that illustrate birds, insects, flowers, cars, Presidents of the United States, historic sites in Canada and Mexico, National folk costumes, Indians of Americas, Japanese rock and roll stars—every conceivable kind of taxonomy. Children who get interested in collecting cards, or in the history of cards, might like to join a card collectors' club. Here are two good ones:

Chicago Playing Card Collectors
1559 West Pratt Boulevard
Chicago, IL 60626

International Playing Card Society
188 Sheen Lane, East Sheen
London SW14 8LF, England

The clubs' regular newsletters will provide information about new decks on the market, card auctions, and people all over the world who want to trade cards.

INTRODUCING THE DECK

There are many ways to introduce a neophyte to playing cards that can teach him the elements of the deck, yet at the same time give him his first taste of the fun, suspense, and sense of order that playing cards can bring. Following are some suggestions.

1. For very young children who may not be able to cope with 52 cards all at once reduce the set. Omit the face cards, leaving 40 cards, from 1 to 10 in 4 suits.

2. Place the deck face down. Let the child remove one card at a time and arrange them in two piles, the reds and the blacks. If he can count, have him see how many there are in each pile. Otherwise, let him try to judge the relative sizes of the piles by measuring them against each other. Can he discover that there are the same number of cards in each?

3. Now see if he can redivide the reds into two piles, each of which has spots of a different shape. Tell him the names of these spots: hearts (already familiar from valentines) and diamonds (as in baseball).

4. Now sort the black ones into two piles and teach the names, the clubs and the spades.

5. Take each of the new groups and arrange in order from one (Ace) to ten. If the child does not yet know number names, have him arrange them in order of density of spots, from the least to the most. Have him array the first sub-set horizontally across the table, and each new one directly below it, so he can note the one-to-one correspondence of cards.

6. Ask him if he can group them a new way, not according to color or shape of marking (suits). If he does not know,

indicate *number*, either the figure in the corner, or the number of suit symbols on the card. Have him group all the 2s together, the 3s together, and so on, until he has ten new sub-sets.

7. See if he can recall all the ways he sorted them. Give him the words to describe what he did: color, suit, number.

8. Introduce the face cards and have him sort them as many different ways as he can, in turn: according to color, according to suit, and according to character. Teach him the names, Jack, Queen, King and help him see the difference between the Jack and King. Direct his attention to the initials on each face card. Have him sort them according to sex (men and women).

ADDITIONAL ACTIVITIES

The following suggested activities are designed to help a child learn or discover the properties of cards. They can be used as supplementary assignments in school settings.

1. Remove one to three cards from the deck and see how quickly, through sorting techniques, the child can name the missing card, or cards. Time him, (for very young or disabled children use a reduced deck, just the face cards or one suit at a time).

2. Have him find out the number of cards of each color (26)
   Have him find out the number of cards of each suit (13)
   Have him find out the number of cards in the deck (52)
   Have him find out the number of cards of each denomination (4).

3. Have him find out which of the groups above can be divided into two even piles.

Which can be divided into three even piles?
Which can be divided into four even piles?

Show him how to divide: deal the cards one at a time into two piles (or three piles) and then continue to place a card on each pile in turn, until that set is exhausted. Does it come out even?

4.   When a whole deck (52) or a deck without face cards (40) is dealt to two people (or into two piles) how many do each get? How many left over? What about four people? Five people? Six people?

5.   Deal out all the cards in horizontal rows, one below the other. How many cards long should the rows be so that there is the same number in each? Can it be done in different ways, say rows of 5, 6 or 7?

6.   How many pairs (two of the same denomination) in the deck? Show the child how to put two together to make a pair and to count all the ones he makes.

7.   Take a complete set of face cards and find out:

> Which King is in profile?
> Which King faces right?
> Which King faces left?
> Which King holds a sword behind his head?
> Which King has a battle-axe?
> Which King holds his sword vertically?
> Which King has no moustache?
> Which Queens face right?
> Which Queens face left?
> Which Queen holds her flower in her left hand?
> Which Queen has a sceptre?
> Which Jacks are in profile?
> Which Jack looks left?
> Which Jack looks right?

Which Jack wears a leaf in his cap?
Which Jack holds a leaf to his lips?
Which Jack has a battle-axe?
Which Jack has no moustache?
Which Jack has two rows of curls?

Since the face cards differ from deck to deck, the teacher may want to make her own list of questions.

8. Introduce children to the Jokers which should be put aside and saved when a new deck is started. If a card is lost (a common occurrence when children play cards) the Joker can be marked and used to take its place, extending the life of the Deck. Some games actually use the Jokers in play (e.g., *Havana*).

Some children have to be taught how to fan the cards in their hand, so that they overlap, and how to hang on to cards in their hands so they do not slip from time to time; and how to hold their hand "close to the vest" so that neighbors cannot peek at their cards. For children who have difficulty and who might become discouraged before they really discover the allure of cards, choose the first games from a group that has few cards to hold, or from a group where hands are not held fanshape (refer to page 53).

There are children who are dextrous enough to hold their cards in a fan-shaped hand but need to be shown *how* to fan their cards. Some (especially left-handed children) fan them to the left and though the hand looks perfectly fine to a player sitting across the table, a peek over the shoulder discloses that the numbers cannot be read. I discovered this when I sat across from a little girl who, from my vantage point, held her hand competently enough, but seemed to be having great trouble choosing a card. I went around to her side of the table to see if I could help her and realized that when cards are fanned to the left—from the lower right corner of the cards—only the number of the top card is visible.

Cards known as "left-handed" or "ambidextrous" cards with numbers in all four corners are available (one source: The Aristera Organization, 9 Rice's Lane, Westport, Conn. 06880). Very clumsy children may be less frustrated in their first efforts at dealing if a reduced deck is used, say, 26 cards. If the number is gradually increased, they can learn to cope with the full deck. In teaching them how to deal, show them that one hand (the nondominant one) is the holding hand and the other is the dealer. Help him learn to use the thumb of the holding hand to feed the cards to the dealer, showing him that if the thumb pushes the card out a little beyond the pack, it is easier for the dealing hand to grasp between thumb and forefinger to pass it out.

I have come across a number of adults who use their left hand to deal, but are right-handed in all other activities. I suspect that some of them may have been natively left-handed, but were encouraged or trained as children to use their right in most situations. Dealing cards seems to escape social control, and a spontaneous choice made early in life sticks with the card player. Watching a youngster whose handedness is uncertain deal for the first few times may help to determine which is his most efficient hand.

There is, in fact, a card dealing test standardized in France used specifically to help determine the dominant hand. ("Handedness Test" by Nadine Galifret-Granjon, described in Zazzo, René, *Manuel pour l'examen psychologique de l'enfant*, Éditions Delachaux and Niestlé, Neuchâtel, Switzerland, 1969, pp. 18-36.) Children are judged by the efficiency with which they handle the cards, the speed with which they deal, the way they use the thumb of the hand that holds the cards. Three trials are given with each hand. The test is based on the assumption that a child, destined to be left-handed, may have been socially conditioned to use his right hand in many activities, but will approach a novel task like card dealing with no social bias. He will discover himself, or with the help of an objective observer, which hand has more facility.

There are many styles of shuffling the cards. Most require considerable finger dexterity. The thumb plays a major role in most versions and must develop enough sensitivity to release the cards smoothly and quickly one at a time, with both hands synchronizing their movements. It is a skill best learned from watching other children, and practiced alone. There is great status in being a good shuffler, and usually enormous motivation to learn. I know several poorly co-ordinated eight- and nine-year old boys who spent hours with cards teaching themselves to shuffle.

44

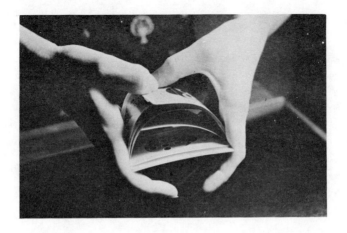

The games described here are games I have played with children, socially and professionally. I have chosen them for their fun and for their educational possibilities. In some cases, these descriptions will differ from those in official rule books. I have outlined them as I learned to play them, and have set down some of the skills each game helps to develop or practice. There are great games that I have left out. *Cribbage, Pinochle, Canasta, Euchre* and some of the innumerable variations of *Poker* and *Rummy* which I know to be good games, are not included because I have never played them with children with learning disabilities. Although there are excellent descriptions in all the compendiums of card games, I felt I should stick to games that I know from experience do the teaching job attributed to them.

Bridge is the most obvious omission. However, Goren can do a much better job at outlining its intricacies. Even though it is a complex game, it has a place in a listing of games for children with learning disabilities. I am thinking particularly of dyslexic teen age boys, with severe reading problems, for whom a long history of academic difficulties and minimal skill at sports has meant relative isolation.

Learning to play Bridge might help their social rehabilitation. I have seen how enthusiastically so called "slow learners" have taken to the game. It does not tax their poor verbal abilities, but still challenges their good intellectual skills. For some, it made them a successful and accepted part of a group for the first time in their lives.

Every teacher and parent will see remedial possibilities in their own favorite games. I hope they will send new ones to me to add to my repertoire.

The age ranges given for each game are only approximate. They include the ages of children that I know have been able to learn and to enjoy playing the games. Some of the simpler games can be made more exciting for older children (beyond the ages given) by introducing poker chips and the element of betting. There will be teachers and parents, I suppose, who disapprove of betting, which smacks of the gambling casino, bookmakers, racetrack, lottery, and other adults follies. But betting is very much a part of children's everyday world, and they turn to it naturally. "I can climb that tree." "I bet you can't." "How much you wanna bet?" In some games (*Poker, Black Jack, Fan Tan, Put and Take,* etc.) the use of chips or other counters is built right in, but

any simple card game is livened up if there are stakes—
something to strive for, and to clearly demarcate the
winner. Betting certainly enhances the possibilities for
teaching mathematics through card games. The betting may
revolve around a point system, counters that are won or
lost, perhaps even exchanged for pennies (20 chips = 1
penny) or candies. In my house, we sometimes play for
chores: the loser has to wipe the dishes, or the winner
doesn't have to make his bed. If you play your cards right,
you can get out of housework altogether.

Listed with each game are the skills that playing helps to
teach, or reinforce, as well as the skills that must be cultivated to play it well. In most cases, I have not mentioned
finger dexterity, rhythm, awareness of direction, visual
scanning, taking turns, and social skills which are practiced
in every game.

For some games, under the heading of "new words" are
reminders to teachers of terms that may be unfamiliar to a
child introduced to the game for the first time, or words
that have an unusual meaning in the context of the game.

To help a teacher or parent choose an appropriate game for
a child or a group of children, the games are listed under
several headings in the next section.

CARD PLAYING CONVENTIONS

Unless specifically cited, the preliminaries to every game are the same, and should be taught so that players, new to cards, learn the most important conventions. These include:

1. Cutting for deal at the beginning of a game. Each player, in turn, takes a stack of cards off the top of the deck, and turns up the bottom card of that stack. Each time he replaces his stack for the next player's cut. The player who turns up the highest ranking card is the dealer.

2. Cutting for partners, where appropriate. The players who have turned up the two highest cards become partners, as do the players who have turned up the two lowest cards.

3. Dealer shuffles the cards before each deal.

4. Player to his right cuts the cards.

5. Cards are dealt from left to right (clockwise)—usually one at a time to each player in turn. Some games specify two at a time, or three at a time.

6. Turn to deal passes to the left.

7. If cards come out uneven, or are inadvertently faced up, it becomes a "misdeal." The dealer shuffles the cards and deals again.

8. Unless specified, cards are picked up and held fan-shaped, so that the other players cannot see what they are.

9. Cards are sorted and arranged according to the demands of the game: in suits, or in groups of the same denomination, or in sequence.

10. It is a card playing custom that players do not pick up their cards until the dealer is ready to do so. Whenever I am

playing with very young children, or with an awkward one, I relax this convention. It speeds up the game if the "slow-pokes" have a chance to sort their cards and get their hands into order while one of the more able players is dealing.

11. If a player makes a mistake—fails to follow suit (in a game like *Hearts*) or to play a required card (say, a 7 in *Fan Tan*), or to produce on request a card he has in his hand (in a game like *Fish* or *Authors*), he is automatically the loser of that hand.

12. Where cards or suits have special rank in play, or special scoring value, it is mentioned. In games like *Fish, Old Maid, Red and Black, Earl of Coventry, Bango,* etc. the cards have no comparative value.

In many games, the cards are ranked according to their number. The Ace functions as *One*. Face cards (Jack, Queen, King) usually have higher rank than any number card. The Queen outranks the Jack, and the King outranks the Queen. In most games, the Ace outranks the King. Some children will be interested to know how it came to be that the lowest card, a one, has the highest value, and outranks even a King. This was not always the case, but developed several hundred years ago, from the democratic notion that the lowest man was more important than the King; so even in cards the lowest became highest.

CARD PLAYERS' VOCABULARY

Following is a list of the terms most common to many card games and used in the directions for play. These should be used in context, so that they become as familiar as household words.

Ace: Card with single mark. Functions as one, or as the card with the highest rank.

Chip in: Contribute counters or chips to a pool.

Cut: Take a stack of cards off the top of the deck. This is usually done by the player to the dealer's right, just before the deal, as a safeguard against cheating (e.g., stacking the deck).

Deal: Hand out the cards to the players, usually one at a time in clockwise rotation, or (as a noun) the act of handing out the cards.

Denomination: The number or face on a card. Two 4s are cards of the same denomination, as are two Jacks, two Kings, etc.

Deuce: The two of any suit.

Discard: (Verb) To get rid of a card as part of the play in some solitaires, or in *Rummy.* (Noun) The card that has been discarded.

Discard pile: See **Trash pile.**

Face cards: Jack, Queen, King (sometimes referred to as "court cards").

Follow suit: Play a card of the same suit as lead player. In some games, players *must* follow suit if they can.

Foundation: Array of cards in solitaires, and in games like *Goof, Fan Tan, Spit,* to be built up or down on in play.

Go out: Be left with no more cards, usually in a game where the first to get rid of all cards is the winner.

Hand: (1) The cards dealt to a player, held in his hand, usually in fan-shaped fashion. In some games, part or all of the hand is face-down or face-up on the table. (2) Players speak of a "good" hand or a "bad" hand, referring to the value of the cards they hold in that particular game. (3) Players talk of "one more hand," meaning another deal and play-out of the cards.

Kitty: See **Pool.**

Layout: A special arrangement of cards on the table required by some games (e.g., *Solitaire, Spit, Havana,* and *Manille*).

Lead: Be the first to play a card in a round of plays.

Meld: To put cards down on the table in acceptable combinations to earn points.

Pass: Pass up the opportunity to bid or to play a card because no suitable play is possible.

Pairs: Two cards of the same denomination.

Pool or Pot: Store of counters or chips contributed to by all the players and won by the winning player.

Run: Three or four cards in sequence as 8, 9, 10; or Jack, Queen, King; or in some games: Queen, King, Ace.

Stock: A pile of cards in the center of the table from which players take cards (draw) when their turns come round.

Suit: The group to which a card belongs, determined by the markings. There are four suits: spades, hearts, clubs, and diamonds. In the standard deck of 52, each suit has 13 cards, from Ace to 10, Jack, Queen, King.

Trash pile: A pile of cards that have been used in play and are no longer required.

Trick: Cards played in turn by each player and won by the player who played the highest ranking card, or in some games, the last card.

Trump: Highest ranking suit, sometimes determined by a card turned over after the deal, or sometimes named by one of the players. In games where there is a trump suit, all trump cards outrank other cards.

Wild: If a card is declared "wild," it is able to stand for any card its holder decides. Rummy is often played with "deuces wild" which means that 2s are premium cards that can fill any slot. In some games that use 53 cards, the Joker is wild. [At one time when playing cards represented the classes of society, the Joker stood for the Court Jester who, as entertainer and social critic, could assume any role.]

GAMES FOR DIFFERENT OCCASIONS

GOOD GAMES FOR TWO

Stinker
Spit
Slap Jack
Go Fish
War
Casino
Kings
Beat the Jack Out of the House
Bow to the King
Concentration
Red and Black
Manille
Up and Down
Crazy Eights
Rummy

FEW CARDS TO HOLD

Fish
Kings
Inflation
Flashlight
Stop and Go
Casino

GAMES THAT NEED NO TALKING

Concentration
Old Maid

Slap Jack
Stinker
Thumbs Down

CARDS NOT HELD FAN SHAPE
(good for children with poor finger dexterity)

War
Black Jack
Beat the Jack
Bow to the King
Concentration
Spit
Pisha Paysha
Slap Jack
Snap
Crazy Eights

FOR VERY YOUNG CHILDREN

Fish
War
Concentration
Inflation
Bow to the King
Bango
Old Maid

GAMES FOR MANY

Bango
Lottery
Havana
Black Jack

GAMES OF CHANCE
(little skill required)

Stop and Go
War
Red and Black
Beat the Jack
Bango
Put and Take
Techtl Mechtl
Earl of Coventry
Crazy Eights

GAMES WITH COUNTERS

Bango
Fan Tan
Lottery
Havana
Black Jack
Macao
Techtl Mechtl
Indian Poker
Put and Take

BETTING

Havana
Black Jack
Macao
Techtl Mechtl
Indian Poker

GAMES WHERE LUCK
AND SKILL COMBINE

Jacks
Hearts
Manille
Oh Hell!
Spit
Fan Tan
Up and Down
Kings
Casino
Twenty-Nine
Black Jack
Macao
Thumbs Down

GAMES OF SKILL

Slap Jack
Bow to the King
Cheat
Concentration
Stinker
Goof

FOR VARIED AGES AND ABILITIES

Havana
Lottery
Earl of Coventry
Techtl Mechtl

GAMES FOR DEVELOPING DIFFERENT SKILLS

FAST VERBAL OR MOTOR REACTION

Slap Jack
Bow to the King
Snap
Animals
Spit
Thumbs Down

LANGUAGE BUILDING

Animals
Bow to the King
Fish
May I
Earl of Coventry
Card Tricks
    Animal, Vegetable, Mineral
    Past, Present, Future
    Penny, Nickel, Dime

THINKING SKILLS

Flashlight
Inflation
Hearts
Doughnut
Manille
Oh Hell!
Rummy
Casino
Card Tricks
    Animal, Vegetable, Mineral
Diversions
    What's My Rule?

MOTOR SKILL

Stinker
Slap Jack
Bow to the King
Spit

SOCIAL SKILLS

Cheat
Casino
Twenty-nine
May I

NOTIONS OF PROBABILITY

Black Jack
Indian Poker
Oh Hell!
Red and Black

NUMERICAL SEQUENCE

Stop and Go
Cheat
Fan Tan
Kings
Up and Down
Spit
Solitaires:
    Clock Solitaire
    Grandfather's Clock
    Threes in a Corner
    Klondike

NUMBER CONCEPTS
(quantity)

War
Indian Poker
Hearts
Inflation
Go Boom
Doughnut

COMPUTATION

Casino
A Hundred and One
Sweet Sixteen
Twenty-nine
Tough Beans
Black Jack
Macao
Rummy
Doughnut
Put-and-Take
Havana
Techtl-Mechtl

Solitaires
    Elevens (A and B)
    Tens
    Ten, Twenty, Thirty
    Thirteen
    Fifteens
    Fourteen
    Pyramid
    Doubles
    Evens
    Odds
    Multiples
    Four Kings

Card Tricks
    Count Down
    Add It Up
    Calculation
    Combinations

VISUAL DISCRIMINATION

Slap Jack
Bow to the King
Concentration
Snap
Bango
Put and Take
Lottery
Authors
May I
Old Maid
Red and Black

VISUAL AND AUDITORY MEMORY

Concentration
Earl of Coventry

RHYTHM

THE CARD GAMES

STINKER

Ages: 4 to adult
Players: 2 to 6

This game is similar to *Jack Straws* or *Pick-Up-Sticks*. It exploits only the physical properties of cards—their lightness, flexibility, and strength—not their numerical properties.

Learning Skills
Helps to develop: • ability to coordinate hand and eye • finger precision and dexterity • a steady hand

First of all. All but five cards of the deck are spread out in a helter-skelter overlapping pile, as level at the center as possible. One player builds a "house" of the five remaining cards on top of the pile. This is made by leaning two cards against each other tent-like, two at the sides, and one across the top.

The object of the game. Is to remove cards from the pile without knocking down the house.

Play. Players take turns in pulling a card from the pile. This is usually done slowly (although not always), using an extended forefinger. The one to knock the house over on his turn is "The Stinker."

At first, players aim for cards that are free of the "house" and have few overlapping cards. Movements must always be steady and smooth. Even leg and body movements must be controlled, because an inadvertent jerk against the table can make the walls of the "house" come tumbling down.

SLAP JACK

Ages: 5 to 12
Players: 2 to 5
(best for 2)

This is often the first card game taught to beginners. Players have only to discriminate Jacks from all other cards. Other denominations are irrelevant, as are suits and ranks. Cards are not held fanshape, so no special finger dexterity is required.

Learning Skills

Helps to develop:
  • visual alertness • quick reactions • fast motor responses • ability to maintain a set*

New word: slap

First of all. The entire deck is dealt one at a time to each player in turn. Each player's cards are left face down in a stack in front of him.

The object of the game. Is to win all the cards. When a player loses all his cards, he may continue to play and to try to win back some cards by being first to slap a Jack. Play continues until one player wins all the cards.

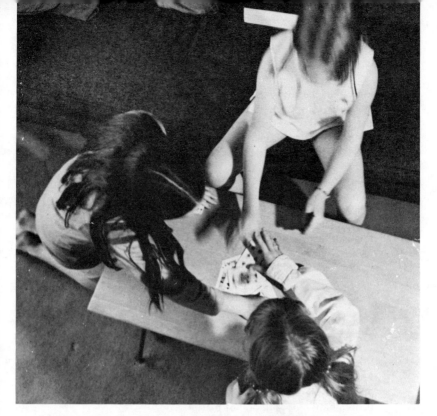

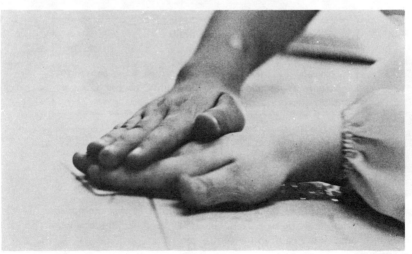

Play. Play begins with the player to the left of the dealer. He turns up a card, and places it quickly in the middle of the table. The next player to the first player's left does the same. Whenever a Jack is played, the first player to slap it takes in the entire pile and places it beneath his stack of cards.

*Comment. Some young players have trouble keeping the object of the game in mind. Having slapped a Jack once, they forget *to get set* to do it again. Games like this help them to learn to hang on to their set to respond in a certain way.

BOW TO THE KING
Ages: 5 to 12
Players: 2 to 5
(best for 2)

This game is easy to learn but some children find it hard to play. Only face cards and Aces must be differentiated; suit, denomination or rank do not matter.

Learning Skills

Good game for developing:
- visual alertness • speedy reactions • the ability to maintain a variable set • the ability to use familiar phrases appropriately and automatically.

First of all. Deck is dealt face down, one card at a time to each of the players in turn from left to right. It does not matter if the deal does not come out even. Each player keeps his cards in a face down stack in front of him.

The object of the game. To be the first to give the appropriate greeting to a Jack, Queen, King or Ace, thereby winning all the cards in the central pile.

To a King—all players bow.
To a Queen—all players say "Good morning, Madam"
To a Jack—all players say "How do you do, Sir"
An Ace—is slapped.

In each case, the first one to give the correct greeting takes in all the cards in the pile and adds them to the bottom of his own stack. If a player gives an incorrect greeting (slaps when he should bow, etc.) he must forfeit a card to the player who played the last card. Winner is the one to end up with all the cards.

Play. Play begins with the player to the left of the dealer. He turns up the top card of his stack and turns it over quickly onto the middle of the table. Cards should be turned over *away* from himself, toward the center of the table. The next player, to his left, does the same.

Suggestions. When there are more than two players, there is often loud controversy over who bowed first, or who spoke first (never over who slapped first, since the evidence of whose hand is on the bottom speaks for itself). Sometimes, it is useful to have one child refrain from playing each hand and act as referee. Learning to accept the judge's decision is an important social lesson.

GO FISH

Ages: 4 to 10
Players: 2 to 5

This is one of the best introductory games. The game is easy to teach and to learn. There are not too many cards to hold or too many variables to cope with; also, a hand does not take too long to play. The suits and ranks of cards are irrelevant; only the notation on each card matters.

Learning Skills

This game is useful for:

● learning number names ● helping to develop the idea of "twoness" (a pair) ● practicing visual discrimination and matching ● left-right discrimination ● the question form "Do you have any . . .?" ● use of plurals ● use of past tense, "I fished upon my wish." ● taking turns

New word: pairs

First of all. Deal six cards to each player. Leave the remaining face down in the center of the table. Players hold their cards in a fan-shaped hand, so that the opponent cannot see what cards they have. Before the play begins, each player checks his hand to see if he has two cards of the same denomination, say two 7s or two Queens.

The object of the game. To get the most pairs. Whenever a player gets a pair, he puts the cards face down in front of him, each new pair overlapping the one beneath it a little, so that they are easily counted at the end of the hand.

Play. The player to the left of the dealer goes first. He asks the player to his left for a card *to match one of the cards in his own hand*, using the formula, "Do you have any [Kings]?" If the player who was asked has one, he must hand it over. The one who did the asking puts down his pair and is entitled to another question. If the player who was asked did not have the card named, he says, "Go Fish," and the first player picks up the top card from the pack in the center. If he gets the card he asked for, he announces, "I fished upon my wish," puts down his pair, and has another turn at asking. He continues to ask as long as he gets what he asked for. If he does not get what he wanted, it is the next player's turn. The deal is over when all cards have been paired. Each player counts his pairs, and the winner is the one with the most.

Modification. This is best played with only two. An adult may play this game with a child who does not know number names. When a young player is asking for a card that matches one of his, he holds his card face up and says, "Do you have any of these?" The adult supplies the label, "Any sixes?" The adult, in turn, when asking, shows the card as he asks, "Do you have any twos?" Because a numeral and a label are repeatedly paired during the game, the child soon learns the names himself.

Developing skill. Though *Go Fish* is mainly a game of chance, there is skill in remembering which cards the player to your left has asked for and did not get. When it is your turn, you can ask for that card if you have it.

AUTHORS

Ages: 5 to adult
Players: 3 to 5

This is a more complicated version of *Go Fish*. Hands are larger. There is more to learn and remember. There is more waiting, and therefore more patience demanded before a player can put down his cards and gain a point. Cards have no rank, but the suits are introduced.

Learning Skills

It is useful for:

• learning number names • learning to discriminate suit markings and learning their names • developing the idea of "fourness" • practicing matching, counting, and polite formula for request, "Please give me . . . ."

New words: book, trick

First of all. All the cards are dealt out, two at a time. It does not matter if the deal does not come out even. Players hold their cards fan-shaped, arranging them so that cards of the same denomination are together.

The object of the game. To collect the largest number of "books" or sets of four cards of the same denomination.

Play. Player to the dealer's left asks any player he chooses for a card by naming a denomination he already has in his hand, but specifying a different suit. He says, "Billy, please give me the [King of clubs]." If the player asked has it, he hands it over and the player whose request was granted gets another turn. If he does not get the card he asks for, the turn to play passes to the player at his left.

As soon as a player collects 4 cards of the same denomination, he lays them face down in front of him as a trick for him.

The game continues until all the cards have been laid down in "books" of four of a kind, and the winner is the one with the most books.

MAY I

Ages: 6 to 12
Players: 3 to 5

This is a version of *Go Fish* which combines some of the elements of *Authors* and some of the elements of the old street game *Giant Step*. *May I* is designed to help children practice some of the useful language formulas. In addition to the same skills as *Go Fish* and *Authors*, children who play *May I* rehearse polite forms of request, acceptance, and refusal (until they are given automatically).

Learning Skills

These are the language forms practiced:
  • "May I have . . .?" • "Yes, you may." • "No, you may not." • "You may have . . . ." • "Thank you." and • "No, thank you."

First of all. All of the cards are dealt two at a time. It does not matter if the deal does not come out even.

The object of the game. To collect the most "books" (tricks) containing sets of four cards of the same denomination.

Play. Player at the dealer's left asks any player he chooses for a specific card, mentioning denomination and suit, saying, "May I have the ___ of _____ (e.g., 3 of diamonds)?" When asking, the first player must have at least one card of the same denomination in his hand. If the player who was asked (second player) has the card, he gives it to the first player, saying, "Yes, you may." Then the first player says, "Thank you." and takes another turn. If the second player does not have the card asked for, he says, "No, you may not, you may have the ___ of _____ [naming the card he has in his hand]." Then, if the first player has a card of the denomination named, he accepts it saying, "Thank you." and takes another turn. If the first player does not have the card offered, he says, "No, thank you." Next, the second player has his turn to ask for a specific card of any player he chooses.

If a player whose request is granted fails to say, "Thank you." he must return the card along with all the cards he has of the same denomination.

If a player fails to say, "No, thank you.", "May I . . .?", "Yes, you may.", or "No, you may not." appropriately, he must give a card from his hand to the other player; the player to receive the card picks it from the other's hand seeing only the backs of the cards (sight unseen).

As soon as a player collects four cards of the same denomination (a book), he lays them down in front of him.

If a player "goes out," that is, has no more cards, his turn to ask goes to the player to his left.

The hand continues until all the cards have been grouped into books. The player with the most books is the winner.

Skill. The skill lies in: (1) Remembering the proper formula for requesting, accepting, or refusing a card. (2) Remembering which cards players have asked for and offered. This increases the chances of asking the right player for the desired card.

70

OLD MAID

Ages: 4 to 10
Players: 2 to 8

This is a popular traditional game that is fun for parents and children to play together. There is a strong element of suspense that keeps everyone involved. For the "liberated" who may find the term "Old Maid" objectionable, the name can be changed to something else more appropriate that has the connotation of odd man out.

Learning Skills

Provides practice in:

    • visual discrimination • matching • recognition of numbers

Helps develop notion of:

    • pairs or "twoness" • taking turns • left-right discrimination • notion of even and odd

New words: pairs, old maid

First of all. Remove the Queen of hearts from the deck and play with 51 cards. Deal out all the cards. For very young children who have trouble holding a fan-shaped hand or more than five or six cards, use a reduced deck, say, a deck of 32 (Ace, King, Queen, Jack through 7) unless you are playing with seven or eight people. When few are playing and the full deck is used (minus the Queen of hearts), deal only six cards to each player and leave the rest as a stock in the middle of the table from which a player can draw each time he puts down a pair.

Each player sorts his cards into pairs of the same denomination—two 3s, two Jacks, etc.—and lays them face down in front of him.

The object of the game. To get rid of all the cards in one's hand by putting them down in pairs, and not to be caught at the end with the odd Queen.

Play. Each player in turn, beginning with the player to the dealer's left, draws a card from the hand of the player to his right. If this gives him a new pair, he lays it down. The play continues until all the cards have been paired off and one player is left with the odd Queen. He loses and becomes the *Old Maid*.

Skill. Though this is largely a game of chance, some players become very adept at "forcing" a Queen on the player who is drawing, by pushing it slightly above the level of the other cards in their fan-shaped hand. The unwary player draws it. Players, in turn, learn to spot the card their opponent wants them to draw, sometimes just by noting the gleam in his eye or the direction of his gaze, and thereby avoiding it.

Variations. (1) Instead of removing the Queen of hearts, one player removes a card from the deck and puts it aside without looking at it. No one knows what the odd card will be, but the holder of the odd card at the end is the *Old Maid*. (2) The Queen of clubs is removed from the deck. Pairs must be of the *same color*. This adds one more variable for a young player to consider. (A 4 of hearts and a 4 of diamonds constitutes a pair since both are red; a King of spades and a King of clubs makes a pair, both black.) The Queen of spades is the Old Maid card and throughout the game, any one who holds it or draws it, is anxious to foist it off on another player.

THUMBS DOWN

Ages: 5 to 15
Players: 3 or more

This is a lively game which offers physical activity to children who cannot sit still for long. It gives children and their teachers the chance to use their ingenuity to create their own variations of the game.

Learning Skills

Helps children practice:

• visual discrimination • categorization • visual alertness • ability to shift set • simple adding • awareness of direction (up, down, left, right) • body awareness

---

First of all. For three players, take the 4 Jacks, Queens, Kings, and the Ace of spades and shuffle them together. For each additional player add a set of four cards. For example, for four players include the four 10s. Deal these cards, one at a time, so that each player has four cards, except the player to the left of the dealer, who has five. Leave the rest of the deck face down in the middle of the table.

The object of the game. To get four of a kind, i.e., a set of four Jacks or four Queens.

Play. Player to the dealer's left passes a card he does not want face down to the player to *his* left who, in turn, picks it up, adds it to his hand, and passes a card face down to the player to *his* left. Player may pass on the card he has just received unless it is the Ace of spades (known as the "bum card"). Play continues until one player has four of a kind. He signals this by making a fist and by turning his thumb down. As soon as the other players notice they must make the thumbs down sign. The last player to do this loses the round. He must pick the top card of the pack. Its denomination determines the number of points that must be credited *against* him. The card is replaced on the bottom of the center pack. The playing cards are shuffled and dealt again for a new hand.

The game continues until one player has 25 points against him and is declared loser.

Variations. To increase the opportunities for developing directional sense, a teacher may suggest varying the signal: (1) Thumbs down, one time; thumbs up, the next; and (2) Player with four of a kind may indicate it by either thumbs down or thumbs up. Other players must copy his signal. The last one to do it correctly loses the round, as above.

To increase opportunities for developing body awareness, a teacher may suggest varying the signal: finger on the nose, touch left ear with right hand, hand on top of the head, etc. One signal is chosen in advance, or first player to go out may choose from a group of predetermined signals, and other players must copy his movement as soon as they see him make it. The last one to do it correctly loses the round, as above.

Spoons. In this version, spoons are placed in the center of the table, one less then the number of players. The first player to get four of a kind grabs a spoon. As soon as they notice this the other players try to get a spoon each. The one left without a spoon loses the round.

In a variation on *Spoons* that helps to develop visual discrimination, there are spoons, forks, and knives on the table, but only the spoons can be used. As before, there is one less spoon than the number of players. A child must make his selection quickly from the array of cutlery before him. Teachers may want to invent their own variations on this, for example, (1) circles, squares and triangles in the center with only the squares as tokens that may be picked up; and (2) a group of cut-out letters or words, only one of which is useable in play.

BANGO

This is a good game for large groups, for players of varied ages and abilities, that demands no special skill, but has the suspense of *Bingo*.

Learning Skills

Playing provides an opportunity:
    ● for learning number names ● for practicing matching ● for practicing counting

New word: caller

Equipment. Two full decks of cards (with backs of different colors) and poker chips or other counters. Players are given an equal number of chips.

First of all. One player is chosen dealer and one player is chosen caller. Dealer deals five cards to each player from one deck.

The object of the game. To be the first to get a chip on every card.

Play. Caller then turns up cards from the other deck, holding them up, and calling them out by denomination and suit (e.g., 4 of clubs). The player who has that card places a chip on it.

The first player to get a chip on every one of his cards calls out, *"Bango."* He names his cards and the dealer checks them out with the cards he has called out. When the hand has been checked, the player who called "Bango" collects all the chips on the other players' cards.

Variation. The game can be made even simpler by leaving out any consideration of suit. Shuffle both decks together.

75

Deal the five cards to each player from the combined deck. Then call the cards by denomination only. For example, if "10" is called, a player may cover one 10 of any suit. If he has two cards of the denomination called, he may cover only one of them, until that denomination is called again.

Modification. When children who do not know number names are playing, Caller should hold up the card for all to see, as he says its name. Children can compare the cards in their hands to the one displayed by the Caller, and cover the matching one.

RED & BLACK

Ages: 4 to 12
Players: 2

Although this is a very simple game, older children seem to be intrigued by it, and often enjoy it more than younger children. This is strictly a game of chance that demands no skill, but it is fun to see the cards roll back and forth between the players.

Learning Skills

Helps children:

• practice classification by color • matching • develop notion of chance and probability

---

First of all. The cards are not dealt. One player holds up the cards, one at a time (with the back of the card to the opposing player) and the other player guesses whether it is red or black. If he guesses correctly, he gets to keep it. In this way, the deck is divided between the two players. Chance sees to it that most of the time each player ends up with approximately half a deck. The players leave their piles face down in front of them.

The object of the game. To win all the cards.

Play. The Guesser turns up a card from the top of his pile to begin a central pile. This is the card to be matched. Each player, in turn, faces up a card on the central pile. The first one to turn up a card of the same denomination as the first one played, takes in the entire pile. Then the other player faces up a new card to be matched and the play continues.

The player to end up with all the cards is the winner.

SNAP

Although this game only requires the players to consider the denomination of the cards, it is nevertheless a game of skill. The skills needed to win are unwavering attention and fast visual and verbal responses.

Learning Skills

Provides practice in:

• visual attention and alertness • visual scanning • visual discrimination • fast verbal reactions • matching

---

First of all. Cards are dealt one at a time to each player in turn and left in a face-down stack in front of each player.

The object of the game. To win all the cards. When a face-down stack is used up, the face-up pile is turned over. If a player loses his cards, he drops out of the game. Winner is the one to capture all the cards.

Play. Each player in turn faces up a card, placing it on a pile in front of his face-down cards. When a card is turned up which is of the same denomination as another card of the top of any player's face-up pile, the first player to say "snap" wins both piles and adds them to the bottom of his face-down stack.

ANIMALS

Ages: 5 to 12
Players: 3 to 6

In this variation of *Snap*, there is one more element to challenge the young player—remembering and giving the correct animal call without hesitation. The game also gives young players an opportunity to exercise their repertoire of animal calls.

Learning Skills

It is a good game for:
- developing visual alertness and visual discrimination
- practicing matching ● developing fast vocal or verbal reactions to a visual stimulus ● encouraging awareness of other players ● stimulating memory

---

First of all. Each player chooses an animal and other players must address him by his animal's call. For example, if he is a cow, other players say "Moo" when the time comes; and if he is a lion, they must roar and so on.

Cards are dealt one at a time to each player in turn and left in a face-down stack in front of each player.

The object of the game. To win all the cards. When a hand is played out, the faced-up pile is turned over and becomes the hand. If a player loses his cards, he drops out of the game.

Play. Each player in turn faces up a card, placing it on a pile in front of his face-down cards. When a player turns up a card which is of the same denomination as another player's face-up card, each player tries to give the animal call of the other player. The one who does it first wins the other player's face-up pile, and adds it to the bottom of his face-down stack.

Variation. Musical instruments: Each player choses a musical instrument and other players must imitate his instrument in sound and gesture at the appropriate time.

THE EARL OF COVENTRY

Ages: 5 to 12
Players: 2 to 6

The engaging rhyme adds a new element to this simple game in which only the numbers and faces of the cards are considered. Suit and rank are irrelevant. The variations demand and help to develop language skill and invention.

Learning Skills

Good game for developing:

• notion of "fourness" • of more and less • auditory discrimination • visual and auditory attention • verbal rhythms • rote memory • language.

First of all. Deal out all the cards to each player in turn. It does not matter if they do not come out even.

The object of the game. Is to be the first to get rid of all the cards in your hand.

Play. Player to the dealer's left plays any card. *Each player must play a card of the same denomination or pass.* As the

first player plays his card, he says, "Here's a '_____'
[naming the card] as good as can be"
The next player says, "Here's another as good as he"
The third says, "Here's the best of all the three"
And the last says, "And here's the Earl of Coventry."

The player who plays the fourth card takes in the cards and leads the next card beginning the rhyme again. Play continues until one player is rid of all his cards and is the winner.

Variations.

1. First player says, "Here's a good [two] from my hand"
   Second player adds, "Here's another that's just as grand"
   Third player adds, "Here is the one to beat the band"
   Fourth player adds, "And here's the best in all the land"!

2. Player who leads may choose the first line of either verse and other players who match his card must give the appropriate follow-up lines.

3. For older players several rhymes (all with the same rhythm) may be used, or players must make up their own as they go along, with the last line always mentioning the Earl of Coventry. For example,

   "I'm giving you my favorite three"
   "Here's another for you from me"
   "Here is mine as you can see"
   "And here's the Earl of Coventry"

or

   "It's my turn to play a nine"
   "If you'll permit me, here is mine"
   "I'm laying one right on the line"
   "The Earl of Coventry's come to dine"

Sometimes the rhymes get pretty silly, as:

"Now I play my diamond King"
"Here is one that likes to sing"
"Here is one that wears a ring"
"The Earl of Coventry, ding, dong, ding"

HAVANA

Ages: 5 to adult
Players: 4 and up

For large groups that vary widely in age and ability, this
game is exciting and fun.

Learning Skills

It is good for:

• developing some prereading skills • recognizing
graphic symbols • visual scanning • developing number
concepts • practicing adding and multiplying • introducing principles of mapping (a printed two-dimensional
representation stands for the actual layout of the cards)

Equipment. Use a 33-card deck: Ace, King, Queen, Jack,
10, 9, 8, 7 of each suit plus a Joker; an equal number of
plastic counters, chips or buttons for each player; a cardboard or paper for each player on which the layout of the
cards is represented as follows:

	A	K	Q	J	10	9	8	7
Spades								
Hearts								
Diamonds								
Clubs								

Each square should be large enough to contain a chip. Children may draw their own betting layouts on a laundry shirt cardboard, or a paper placemat, and once drawn, they can be saved from game to game.

First of all. The dealer-banker lays out 4 rows of 8 cards each, face down, and the last card is set aside. Then he calls for bets. The players place bets. They are betting that certain cards will be turned up. They may bet on as many individual cards as they choose by placing a chip or more in the square that represents each card; they may bet on vertical rows of four cards (say, all the Aces), placing a chip or more below the column of their choice; they may bet on horizontal rows of eight cards (say, all the clubs) by placing their bet in the square at the end of the row.

Showdown. When the bets have been placed, the last card is turned up. Dealer places this in the correct place on the layout (as designated on the player's cardboard). For example, if it is the Ace of spades, it takes the places of the first card in the first row. All bets made on that card are paid. The card it displaces is then faced up and placed correctly.

Again, bets are paid and a new card is faced up. The play continues in this way until the Joker is faced up which ends the *Showdown.* If the Joker is turnedup first, as the 33rd card, the Banker collects all the bets.

Pay-offs. On any card faced up each player is paid the amount of his bet. If a column is bet on and faced up, the Banker pays four times the bet. If a row is bet on and faced up, the Banker pays eight times the bet. The Banker collects all unsuccessful bets.

PUT & TAKE

Ages: 5 to adult
Players: 3 to 8

This is another game that is good for players of all ages. The youngest will need help in settling and paying their bets, but should have no other difficulties. Only the numbers of the cards are relevant to the game.

Learning Skills

May be used for practicing:
- matching ● counting ● multiplying (doubling)

Equipment. Full deck of cards and poker chips. Players are equipped with an equal number of chips.

First of all. The dealer gives 5 face-up cards (one at a time) to each player except himself.

Play. Then the dealer begins to deal himself a hand of 5 cards one card at a time. Each player who has a card of the

same denomination as the dealer's first face-up card, puts 1 chip into the pot for each one he has. Each player holding cards to match the second of the dealer's cards puts in 2 chips for each; 4 chips for each card of the same denomination as the dealer's third card; 8 chips for the fourth card; and 16 chips for the fifth card.

Showdown. Now the dealer begins dealing himself a new hand of 5 cards. This time, players holding cards of the same denomination take chips out of the pool. One for each card that matches dealer's first card; 2 for each card that matches dealer's second card; 4 for the third; 8 for the fourth; and 16 for the fifth. Dealer must make good any chips coming to a player, and takes any chips left in the pot after all claims are settled.

LOTTERY

Another game to accommodate everybody. In this game, number and color are relevant, but not suit or rank.

Learning Skills

Good game for practicing:
   ● visual discrimination ● visual scanning ● counting ●
dividing ● keeping several variables in mind

Equipment. Two decks of 52 cards and plastic counters.

First of all. There are two dealers, one for each deck. The first dealer deals one face-down card to each player. Each player places an equal bet (previously decided on) on his card.

85

Showdown. Second dealer takes the other deck and deals one face-up card to each player. Players then expose their face-down card. If a player's face-down card matches any face-up card in denomination, he wins the chips on that card. If there is more than one winner, the chips are divided. If the face-down card also matches a face-up card in color, the player who has it must pay an extra chip. If a player's face-down card matches his own face-up card, he collects his own stake as well as an extra chip from each player.

Any chips not collected are left on that player's card for the next deal, along with the new stakes each player must put up.

TECHTL-MECHTL

Sometimes called, "The Ninth Card," this is a superb betting game for groups whose ages and abilities vary widely. Both number and suit of cards are relevant.

Like all gambling games, Techtl-Mechtl is good for practicing arithmetic, especially multiplication. The possibilities for practicing arithmetic are enhanced if the game is played with plastic counters and they are given different values, say blue = 10¢, red = 5¢, white = 1¢ and if different bets are permitted.

Learning Skills

Good for:

 • visual discrimination • keeping several variables in mind • practicing arithmetic computation.

Equipment. Two decks of 32 cards (Ace, King, Queen, Jack, 10, 9, 8, 7 in each suit). For 6 players: leave in the 6s. For 5 players: leave in the 5s and 4s. For 8 or more players: use complete deck of 52. Counters: preferably of different colors.

First of all. Players take equal amounts of chips. The dealer-banker puts into the bank (pot) an amount decided on before the deal. Each deck is used separately: one for the deal and one for the "showdown."

Deal. Dealer-banker gives each player in turn, as many cards (from 1 to 6) as the player is prepared to bet on. Players tell dealer how many to deal. Players may vary their bets on each card, arranging and separating the cards to indicate their bets: cards closest to the player which are arranged vertically, side by side, indicate 1¢ bets; cards arranged horizontally, after these, indicate 5¢ bets and cards closest to the bank, arranged vertically indicate 10¢ bets. The chips bet are placed in the pot along with the dealer's initial investment.

Showdown. Dealer-banker takes the second deck (cut first, of course, by the player to his right) and faces up the bottom card. Any player with this card can trade it for another from the top of the first deck.

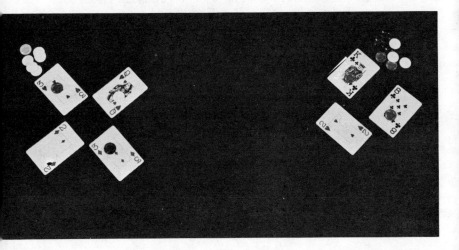

Then, two cards from the top of the second deck are faced up and placed side by side. Neither of these is a paying card, and any player having *identical* cards (in both suit and denomination) may again turn them in and have them replaced by cards from the top of the first deck (the original bets made remain constant).

The banker-dealer then faces up two new cards, placing them below the first two. Any player who holds an identical card collects from the bank, double the bet he placed on it.

Next, two new cards are faced up in a third row. A player with an identical card collects triple the bet he placed.

Then, two new cards are faced up in a fourth row, and any player holding either of them collects four times his bet.

Finally, the ninth card is faced up and placed horizontally below the four rows, to signify the end of the showdown. The player holding this card collects nine times his bet.

Any counters left on the players' cards go into the bank.

If, at any time, the bank is "broken" (that is, there are no more chips to pay off bets), the turn for dealer-banker passes to the left. Otherwise, the dealer-banker continues until the bank contains an amount equal to three times the banker-dealer's original investment. Then he gives notice that he will deal only one more time. He can keep whatever is left in the bank after the next deal and showdown. Players can never collect more than the amount in the bank and the dealer-banker is never personally liable.

Comments. Although young children often will need help with the calculations, they nevertheless enjoy the chance to be dealer-banker. Even if they have never learned to multiply, they soon understand the relative increase in quantity that two times, three times, four times, and nine times bring.

CONCENTRATION

Ages: 4 to adult
Players: 2 to 6

This is an excellent introductory game. For some reason very young children often amaze adults with their unusual playing skill.

Learning Skills

This game:

• provides practice in matching • helps teach the notion of pairs • helps develop visual alertness, visual memory, and awareness of position

---

First of all. The entire deck is dealt out face down on the table. (The game is easier (at least for adults) when the cards are arranged in rows, but this is not essential.)

The object of the game. To collect the most pairs. As long as a player draws pairs he continues to play. If the cards do not match, they are faced down again and the next player draws two cards. Play continues until all the cards have been paired. Winner is the one who has taken in the most cards.

Play. Each player, in turn, faces up two cards. If they match (are the same denomination) he takes them in as his pair and gets another turn.

Comments. The skill lies in paying close attention to each player's turn and noting and remembering the cards that have been faced-up and their position. The skillful player, on turning up a card of a denomination that has appeared before, will immediately know where to reach for a matching card.

When the cards are arranged in rows, players with poor ability for visual recall, can be taught to use verbal cues to help them hang on to what they saw: e.g., "fourth row, second card—3". They can even draw the cards of their first few turns in a systematic order, say all the cards in the first row, and memorize the order (e.g., "King, 10, 4, 8 . . ." by rehearsing it mentally until it sticks.

BEAT THE JACK
OUT OF THE HOUSE

In this game, the idea of *high cards* (some cards outranking others) is introduced.

Learning Skills

Playing the game gives practice in:
- taking turns ● simple counting ● visual alertness

Rank of cards. Ace, King, Queen, and Jack outrank all other cards.

First of all. Deck is divided into two stacks with cards faced down in a pile in front of players.

The object of the game. To win all the cards by turning up high cards.

Play. Cards are faced up by each player in turn, one at a time, on a pile in the center. Player who plays a face card or Ace is eligible to take in the pile, *but* his opponent is given a chance to try to beat his card by playing additional cards:

On a Jack—one card
On a Queen—two cards
On a King—three cards
On an Ace—four cards

If any one of these is a face card, he immediately stops adding cards and the opponent takes the same privileges, playing one card on a Jack, two on a Queen, three on a King, or four on an Ace. If none of these is a face card or Ace, the last player to have played one of the high ranking cards wins the pile, adds it to his own, and the play resumes. The player to get all the cards is the winner.

THREE
CARD MONTE

This is a version of the old "Shell Game" dedicated to the notion that the hand is quicker than the eye. Players have a chance to challenge that notion, while developing skill and speed in both hand and eye. Dealer can practice fast, smooth, coordinated hand movements. Bettors get practice in visual tracking, sorting out figure from ground.

Learning Skills

Helps to develop awareness:

• develop awareness of number and one-to-one correspondence • to practice counting.

Equipment. Three cards: Ace of spaces, Ace of hearts, Ace of diamonds; equal number of poker chips for each player.

First of all. Dealer takes his three cards, shows them one at a time to the other players and lays them face down on the table. Then using both hands, he mixes them, rearranging

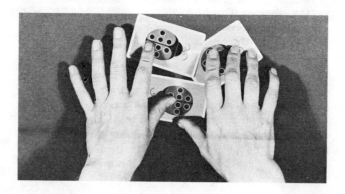

them by pushing them about on the table top with a few quick moves.

Play. Players then place bets on the card they think is the Ace of spades.

Showdown. Cards are faced up. Dealer must pay an amount equal to the bet of those who bet correctly. Dealer collects unsuccessful bets.

WAR

Ages: 5 to 12
Players: 2

In this game only the denomination of the cards matters. Since this is strictly a game of chance, requiring no special skill, all players are on an equal footing.

Rank of cards. Ace is highest, then King, Queen, Jack, 10 down to 2.

First of all. Deck is divided evenly into two stacks, and each player keeps his cards in a face-down stack in front of him.

The object of the game. To get all the cards.

Play. Both players together turn their top card up. The player playing the highest card takes in both cards and adds them to his stack, putting them on the bottom or to the side face down. If players face up cards of the same denomination, it means WAR. Spelling aloud, "W-A-R", as they place them, they play three face-down cards on their top card, then as a fourth card is played face up, they say "War!" The player of the highest faced-up card takes all the cards. Or, if they are again of the same denomination, the "W-A-R—War" play is repeated. The play continues until one player gets all the cards and is the winner.

Variation. *Liberation:* some may think that it is unfair that the Queen should be lower in rank than the King. This game might be a good place to introduce the notion of equal rank. If a Queen and King are turned up simultaneously, then it's "War!"

Learning Skills

Children playing get practice in:

● simple counting ● learning to judge numerical value (higher and lower numbers) ● rhythm (synchronizing movements with other players)

New words: high and low

FLASHLIGHT

This is the only game I know of where only the *suits* of the cards are relevant. For this reason it makes a good introduction to the principle of classifying cards by suits.

Learning Skills

Useful for practicing:
   ● matching ● classification or categorization ● visual alertness ● keeping a secret

---

First of all. Dealer deals seven cards to each player. The rest of the pack is not used. Cards are held in the hand, fan-shaped, so the other players cannot see them.

The object of the game. To be the first to have all your cards of the same suit.

Play. The dealer begins. He takes any one of his cards that he does not want and lays it *face down* in front of the player to his left.

That player, before looking at the card, takes one of *his* cards and lays it face down in front of the player at his left, and so on around the table. Each one always puts one card face down in front of the next player *before* looking at the card he has been given.

The first player to get seven cards of the same suit calls, "Flashlight," and wins the game.

Comments. Players should try to go for the suit they have most of to start with. Also, young children should be cautioned to not let anyone know what suit they are saving.

GO BOOM

This game, where denomination, suit, and rank are all considered, introduces youngsters to the principle of following suit, and of taking in tricks with a high card (common to many more complicated card games).

Learning Skills

Good game:

• for practicing matching both suit markings and numbers • for developing notion of "higher," "lower," "greater," smaller," • for learning to judge numerical rank • for categorizing

New words: follow suit, highest card

Equipment. Full deck of 52 cards. If more than six play, use two decks.

Rank of cards. Ace (high), King, Queen, Jack down to 2 (low).

First of all. Dealer deals seven cards to each player one at a time in turn. The rest of the deck is left in a face-down stack in the center.

The object of the game. To get rid of all the cards in your hand.

Play. The first player (player to the left of the dealer) leads any card. Each player in turn must follow suit. If he cannot play a card of the same suit, he may play a card of the same denomination as the last card played. If he can do neither, he draws from the stack in the center, one at a time, until he can play. If there are no more cards in the center and he still cannot play, he misses his turn, and the next player makes his play. The player who has played the highest card

of the suit that was led, takes the trick in, and leads to the next trick (begins the next round of plays).

As soon as a player gets rid of all the cards in his hand, he calls "Boom!" and is the winner.

INFLATION

Ages: 6 to adult
Players: 2 to 6

An easy game for introducing the idea of following suit and taking in tricks with the highest card.

Learning Skills

Playing the game provides practice in:

● categorizing ● understanding the comparative value of numbers and notions of rank order ● finger dexterity (required to hold the large number of cards a player can accumulate) ● visual scanning

New words: follow suit, highest card

Equipment. A 32-card deck: Ace, King, Queen, Jack, 10, 9, 8, 7 in each suit (for up to four players); for five players, add 6s and 5s; for six players, add 4s and 3s.

Rank of cards. Ace (high), King, Queen, Jack down to 2 (low).

First of all. Each player is dealt eight cards—three, two, three at a time.

The object of the game. To be the first player to get rid of your cards.

Play. The first player leads any card. Each player in turn must follow suit. If all follow suit the one who plays the highest card takes in the trick and leads to the next one.

If a player cannot follow suit, he must pick up all the cards already played to that trick and add them to his hand. He then leads to the next trick and the play continues. The first player to get rid of all his cards wins the game.

PISHA PAYSHA

Ages: 5 to 12
Players: 2

The pace of the play as the players synchronize their playing rhythm with each other gives this game its own special appeal.

Learning Skills

This is a good game for:
● practicing matching and categorizing ● judging numerical value ● developing rhythm

---

Rank of cards. Ace (high), King, Queen, Jack, 10 down to 2 (low).

First of all. The entire deck is dealt out and each player keeps his cards in a face-down stack in front of him.

The object of the game. To get all the cards. The first player to do so is the winner.

Play. Each player keeps turning up cards—at the same rate as his opponent—on a pile in front of him. When both players simultaneously turn up cards of the same suit, the player with the highest ranking card takes in all the cards in his opponent's face-up pile.

When there are no more cards in the face-down pile, the face-up pile is turned over and the play continues.

CRAZY EIGHTS

Ages: 5 to 12
Players: 2 to 6

In this game both suit and denomination are taken into consideration. Cards have no special rank, but the Jack, 8 and 2 are treated differently. *Crazy Eight* hands often get very large and players must frequently scan their hands to see if they have a card they can play. The large hands require considerable finger precision to keep them all fanned out. Children are introduced to the notion of a "wild" card.

Learning Skills

It provides practice in:
● flexibility (changing your set whenever it is necessary ● visual discrimination and scanning ● finger dexterity

---

First of all. Deal eight cards to each player. The remaining cards are placed in the middle, and the top card of the deck is turned up beside it.

The object of the game. To be the first to get rid of all your cards.

Play. The first player must place on top of the turned-up card a card of the same suit, or a card of the same denomination, or an 8. If he plays an 8, he can declare it any suit he chooses, that is, the "wild" card. Each player, in turn, must match the faced-up card as to suit or denomination, or play an 8. If he has no playable card to play, he draws cards from the pack until he gets one.

If a player plays a Jack, he may put another card on top of it (but, of course, it must be of the same suit, or denomination, or an 8). If he tops it with another Jack, he plays again.

If a player plays a 2, all the other players must each pick up two cards from the face-down pack and add them to their hands.

When all the pack has been faced up, cards are shuffled and turned over again. The last played card is left face up to be played upon.

Comments. Many of the children I know who play this game enjoy switching the wild card periodically. Usually the winner of a hand announces the new wild card for the next hand, by saying "crazy sevens" or "crazy tens" or whatever. This forces the players to remember the wild card, to be even more flexible in their approach to the game, and to be additionally vigilant.

INDIAN POKER

This game provides children with a good introduction to the sport of betting and calculating probabilities. The game compels the child to guess, but has in it the elements that allow him to make a calculated guess.

Learning Skills

Helps to teach:

● simple counting ● notions of highest, lowest, and middle ● probabilities

New words: highest, lowest, in the middle

Equipment. Deck of 52 cards and an equal number of poker chips for each player.

First of all. Dealer gives each player one card face down.

Play. Without looking at his card, each player holds it against his forehead, so that he cannot see what it is, but the other players can.

Betting. Each player, starting with player at dealer's left puts equal number of chips into the pot (say, two or four

so the total will be divisible by two, in case of a tie) and after looking over his opponents' two cards, bets whether his card is highest, lowest, or in the middle.

Showdown. Players look at their own cards and the one who correctly named his card's status (highest, lowest, or middle) collects the pot. If more than one player was correct the chips are divided. If there were no correct bets the chips remain in the pot for the next deal (though players bet again with each deal). After bets are collected, the deck is shuffled, and the next player in turn deals.

Variation. Cards are collected after each deal, and placed face up on the bottom of the deck. A new deal is begun from the top *without shuffling* until the deck is exhausted. Thus, players who can remember the cards that have appeared can bet with increasingly greater assurance as they get further into the deck. Teenagers find this variation very challenging. It stimulates memory, reasoning ability, and mathematical logic.

UP & DOWN

Numerical sequence, regardless of suit, and numerical sequence within suits are the important considerations in this game.

Learning Skills

The game provides practice:

• in placing numbers in sequence, both up and down the number line • in categorizing • in maintaining a variable set

---

First of all. Deck is dealt out between the two players. Cards are left in a face-down pile before each player.

The object of the game. To be first to get rid of all your cards.

Play. Players take turns facing up their cards—one at each turn—onto a pile in front of their face-down stacks. If a card is an Ace it is put in the center of the table. Cards faced up may be played to the center (building upwards in suit sequence on the Aces) or on an opponent's face-up pile in sequence, *up or down* regardless of suit. Thus, if one player has a Queen on the top of his face-up pile, the other player may place any Jack or King; if he has a 5 on top, any 4 or 6 may be played on it.

If a faced-up card can be played, either to the center or on opponent's pile, player can have another turn, and continue to face up cards until he can make no more plays. The top card of the face-up pile is always available for play.

When the face-down stack is exhausted, the face-up pile is turned over and play continues.

GOOF

Ages: 5 to adult
Players: 2 to 6

This game encourages players to be alert. During his own turn, a child tries to exploit every possible play or else one of his opponents can score a point against him. During his opponent's turn, he should watch for misplays or missed opportunities and thereby gain an advantage.

Learning Skills

Good game for practicing:
- numerical sequence (up and down) • principles of alternation • visual scanning • visual alertness • shifting sets

---

Equipment. Deck of 52 cards.

First of all. Dealer deals out all the cards to each player in turn except four which are placed face-up in the center as foundation cards. Cards are kept in face-down stacks in front of each player.

The object of the game. To be first to get rid of your cards.

Play. Player faces up top card from his pile beginning a face-up pile. Any Ace that is faced up is played *above* the foundation cards. Cards from face-up pile may be played on Aces in *upward* sequence of the same suit. Cards may be played on foundation cards in *downward* sequence, alternating colors (e.g., black 9 on red 10); or on any opponent's face-up card in *upward or downward* sequence or alternating color. A player may play onto the Aces from the foundation, move cards from one foundation pile to another to release cards to be played on the Ace pile, move *entire* foundation piles to another when possible, and fill in blank spaces in the foundation row. A player continues to face up cards from his stack until he can make no more plays. Then the next player begins. If a player misses a possible play, plays incorrectly or out of turn, one of his opponents can call "Goof!" and the player who goofed must take the top card from that opponent's face-up pile, and add it to his own face-up pile.

Summary of possible plays: 1. Downward sequence on foundation cards, alternate colors. 2. Upward sequence on Aces of same suit. 3. Upward or downward sequence (alternate colors) on opponent's pile. 4. The top card from foundation pile or entire pile can be played on other foundation piles or opponent's pile. 5. Cards from own pile or other foundation cards onto empty foundation spaces (after one of the entire foundation piles is removed).

KINGS

Also called, "Four Corners." The color of the cards, and their position in numerical sequence are the important variables here.

Learning Skills

The game provides practice in:
● alternation (red on black; black on red) ● placing numbers in downward sequence ● visual alertness

---

First of all. Seven cards are dealt to each player. The rest of the deck is put in the middle face down, and the four top

106

cards are turned face up on four sides of the center pile. If two of them are of the same denomination, the last one played is put back into the stack, and replaced with a new card from the top. Similarly if one of them is a King, it is put back in the deck, and is replaced. These four cards around the deck constitute the layout piles. The four corners are reserved for Kings.

The object of the game. The first player to play out all his cards (including the one he has drawn from the stock) is the winner.

Play. Each player in turn draws one card from the deck and then plays as many cards as he can on the layout piles, placing cards one lower in sequence, and of an alternate color. For example, if the layout cards include a 3 of spades, and a Jack of diamonds, a player can put any red 2 on the 3, any black 10 on the Jack, followed by a red 9, and a black 8, if he has them. He can play as many suitable cards as he has in his hand.

A layout pile can be moved to another pile if its bottom card (card at the top of the sequence) can be suitably placed on one of the others. If, for example, one of the piles has red 10, black 9, red 8, black 7, red 6, built down in sequence, and another pile has red Queen, black Jack, then the red 10, and all the cards on it, can be put on the black Jack. The player who does this can fill in the empty space in the layout with a card from his own hand.

If a player has a King, he places it in a corner, and this begins a new layout pile, to be built upon in descending sequence—alternating colors as in the other piles. If it is completed, from King down to Ace, it is turned over.

FAN TAN

Suits and numerical sequence of the cards are considered in play.

Learning Skills

Players get practice:

• in categorizing (cards are grouped into suits) • in arranging numbers in sequence—both upward and down-ward • in simple counting • visual scanning in both vertical and horizontal planes • in developing strategies

New words: up and down

Equipment. Deck of 52 cards; an equal number of chips for each player.

First of all. The full deck is dealt out to the players. In the course of play, a layout will be laid out consisting of 3 piles in 4 horizontal rows—a row for each suit. The center

108

vertical column is for 7s. On the right of each 7, the 8 of the same suit is placed. On the left of the 7 go matching 6s. On the 8s, players play cards of the same suit building up in ascending sequence to King. On the 6s players build down in descending suit sequence to Ace.

The object of the game. To be the first to play out all your cards.

Play. The first player must begin the layout with a 7 or forfeit a chip to the pot. Until a 7 of a suit is played, no other card in that suit may be played. After the 7 of a suit is played, the matching 6 or 8 may be played, and the players may begin playing appropriate cards on them (a 9 on the 8, or a 5 on the 6, etc.). Each player, in turn, must play a 7 or add a card to the layout. If he cannot he puts a chip in the pool.

The player to get rid of his cards first is the winner of the hand and of all the chips in the pool. Players must pay him one chip for each card they hold in their hands.

Variation. This game may be played two-handed. Deal seven cards to each player. Leave the rest of the cards face down as a stock. When a player cannot play he draws a card from the stock. If he still cannot play, he pays a chip to the pool, and draws again. He repeats this until he can play.

Comments. Toward the end of each hand players can learn to choose carefully among the possible plays. Playing certain cards may permit the opponent to win or "go out." A player can develop the ability to guess which cards his opponent is holding, to withhold a card that will help him, and to play one that will be to his own advantage.

CHEAT

Sometimes called "I Doubt It." While playing or pretending to play cards in numerical sequence, children are introduced to the fine art of bluffing.

Learning Skills

Players practice:
   • numerical sequence • counting • gauging probabilities • reading facial expressions • controlling their own facial expressions • keeping track of what has happened

---

Rank. Cards have no comparative value, but go in sequence from Ace through to King, and back to Ace repeating the sequence.

First of all. All the cards are dealt out. Players hold their cards in fan-shaped hands.

The object of the game. To be the first to get rid of all your cards.

Play. First player puts 1 to 4 cards, *face-down*, on the table, announcing their denomination; for example, two 3s, or 4 Jacks, or whatever. He may be telling the truth or lying. Next player, in turn, must play, or pretend to play one to four cards next in sequence, announcing (if previous player has called "3s", for example) "two 4s". Any player who doubts a declaration may call "cheat!" and the last cards played are inspected. If the cards are not the ones he claimed, the player who played them must pick up all the cards on the table and add them to his hand. If they are the cards that were announced, the player who called "cheat" must pick up all the cards on the table and add them to his hand. The player who was correct (who played what he said, or who correctly detected "cheating") resumes the play by starting a new sequence.

Play continues until one player gets rid of all his cards, and is declared winner. Some children like to continue the game letting the winners drop out, until one player is left with all the cards, and is the loser.

In some cases each player pays the winner one chip for every card he has left in his hand.

Comments. This game is also called *"I doubt it,"* which is used instead of *"cheat."* All of the children I know prefer "cheat," (because of its blunt, straight-forward rudeness, I suppose). A teacher, who wanted to help a group of children learn and practice a polite formula of disagreement, could introduce the game as "I doubt it," or "I beg your pardon" or "Would you mind if I looked at your cards?".

STOP & GO

Numerical sequences (the order of the cards from Ace through to King) and their suits are the considerations in playing this game. It is a very good game for children who are in the process of learning to count.

Learning Skills

Opportunities to practice:
  • categorizing • numerical sequence

New word: stop

First of all. When four play: twelve cards are dealt to each, and the four remaining cards are left aside face down as "stops." For three players: fifteen cards each, and seven stops; for five players: nine cards each, and seven stops; for six players: eight cards each, and four stops. Cards are held fan-shape by each player.

The object of the game. To be first to get rid of all the cards.

Play. First player leads any card face up, saying its number aloud, e.g., "two." The player to his left must follow with the next card in sequence of the same unit. If he has it, he plays it, calling "three." If he does not have it, he says "pass." Each player who does not have it, passes in turn until someone who can play it does. The sequence continues until it reaches a *Stop*, (that is, when no player has the next card because it is in the face-down Stop pile, or the card last played is a King). The player of the last card begins a new sequence by playing any card.

The first player to get rid of his cards wins the game.

SPIT

This is a game that seems to be more familiar to children then to adults. It is passed from child to child, rather than from adult to child (like *Go Fish* or *Concentration*). The only adults I know who can play the game have learned it from their children. It can go on for hours and this may be one of the reasons children love it. This is a fast game and a good one for helping a child develop quick responses. Even the day dreamers seem to pick up speed when they play *Spit*.

Learning Skills

Practice in:

● left to right progression ● visual scanning and visual alertness ● counting ● maintaining a variable set (keeping several ideas in mind at once) ● number sequence (up and down) ● fast motor reactions

---

First of all. The deck is divided evenly between both players. Players face each other. Each player deals out the following layout: a row of five cards, the first card of which is face up, the next four face down. Then from the remaining stack, turn one card face up and place it on the second card in the row and cover the next three with face-down cards. Then turn another card from the stack face up and put it on the third pile in a row, and cover the next two piles with face-down cards. Then turn another card face up and put it on the fourth pile in the row and cover the last pile with a face-down card. Then face up the last card and place it on the fifth pile.

The object of the game. To be first to get rid of all the cards. The object of each hand is to be the first to get rid of all the cards in the layout—thus, plays are made as quickly as possible.

Play. The players hold the remaining cards face down in the palm of their hands. Then the players say together "One-two-three-Spit" and both face up a card between their two layouts. The *"Spit" cards* are to be "built on"—up or down, with cards of any suit from each player's layout. For example, if one of the Spit cards is the 10 of diamonds, players can put on a Jack of any suit, or a 9 of any suit, and continue to build on the new card in either direction.

As top cards in the *layout* piles are put on the Spit cards, the card underneath is face up. As positions in the layout become vacant, a card can be taken from the top of any pile, and put in the empty space. When neither player can make a play on the Spit cards, the players prepare to put down new Spit cards (on the existing Spit card pile), saying again, "One-two-three-Spit!" and the race to get rid of cards by building begins again.

If a player runs out of Spit cards he may borrow three from his opponent to be paid back later.

The play continues until one of the players has no more cards in his layout pile. The winner then chooses the smallest of the two Spit piles (he may not count cards, but he is allowed to compare the two piles). The opponent takes the other pile, and with these as their decks, the play resumes. Each player shuffles his cards, and lays them out as he did originally. If a player does not have enough cards to complete the original layout, that is, fewer than 15, he makes five piles, but with fewer cards in the last two or three piles.

Play continues until one player has no more cards. Since the game can go on for hours without an out-and-out

winner, players can set a time limit. Winner is the one with the fewest cards at the end of the game.

Comments. Skillful players keep an eye on the opponent's layout, and near the end of the game will withhold a card that will give the opponent a chance to go out.

Variation. *Horse Spit* (probably modified by children for play in cramped quarters; the back seat of a car; or when an orange crate serves as a table): Layout consists only of four piles, laid out exactly as in Spit. Aces are *wild*. *Bank*: played exactly as Spit, but the object of the game is *to get* all the cards. Therefore, winner of each hand chooses the *largest* Spit pile to add to his cards.

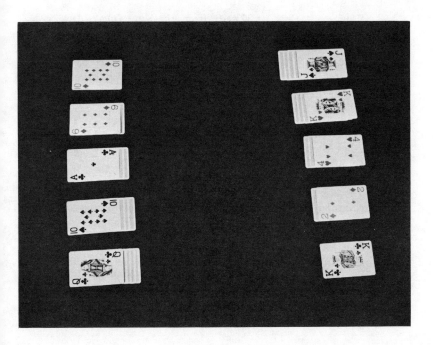

JACKS

This is a good introduction to the principle of *avoiding* key cards. It is simpler than *Hearts*, but a good preliminary to learning Hearts. Suit and rank are relevant.

Learning Skills

This game helps to provide practice in:

• counting • adding • categorizing • judging quantitative rank of numbers • remembering • calculating probabilities • developing strategies

---

Equipment. Deck of 32 cards from Ace, King, Queen, Jack, 10 through 7. When 5 or 6 play remove the black sevens.

First of all. The entire deck is dealt out, so that each player has the same number of cards. Cards are held fan-shape, so opponents cannot see the cards. Players sort their cards into suits.

Point value. Jack of clubs, hearts, diamonds each count as a point against the player who takes it in. Jack of spades counts as 2 points against him.

The object of the game. To avoid taking in tricks with counting cards *or* to take in all the tricks with counting cards.

Play. First player leads a card. Everyone must follow suit. If a player has none of the suit led, he can play any card, this may be his chance to get rid of a Jack or a high card. The person who played the highest card takes in the trick and leads for the next trick. Play continues until all the cards are played out.

At the end of the hand the points are counted, and may be recorded on a score sheet.

The deck is shuffled, and the deal passes to the left for a new hand.

The game is played until one player has ten points against him, and is declared loser.

HEARTS

Ages: 7 to adult
Players: 3 to 5

This is a game of skill that appeals to youngsters but provides a challenge for even the most experienced adult. Suit and rank are both relevant.

Learning Skills

Provides practice in:

● categorizing ● counting ● judging quantitative rank of numbers ● considering several factors at once ● maintaining variable set ● adding (including adding negative numbers) ● reasoning ● memory ● calculating probabilities ● developing strategies

New words: control, against

First of all. The entire deck is dealt out, so that each player has the same number of cards. With three players remove the 2 of diamonds from the deck; with five players remove the 2 of diamonds and the 2 of clubs. Cards are held fan-shape, so opponents cannot see the cards. Players sort their cards into suits.

Point value. Every heart counts one point against the player who takes it in and the Queen of spades sometimes known as "Maggie" counts thirteen points against the player who takes it in. Unless the player gets *"control." Control* is getting all thirteen hearts, and the Queen of spades in your tricks. When this happens, all other players get 20 points counted against them.

The object of the game. To avoid taking in tricks with counting cards *or* to take in all the tricks with counting cards.

Play. First player leads a card. *Everyone must follow suit.* If he has none of the suit led, he can play any card. The person who played the highest card takes in the trick and leads for the next trick. Play continues until all the cards are played out.

At the end of the hand the points are counted and recorded on a score sheet. The deck is shuffled, and deal passes to the left for a new hand.

The game is played until an agreed number of points is reached. Winner is the player with the least points.

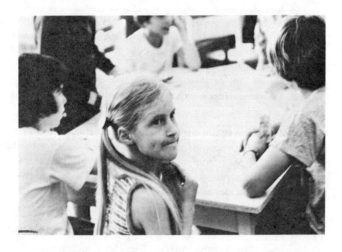

MANILLE

Manille (pronounced manee) was taught to me by a boy from Belgium. The North American youngsters I know were not familiar with it. I have taught it to many children who have loved it. It challenges the intellect, there are many opportunities for strategic play, and the game is full of surprises. Because it is played with a 32-card deck, it is easier to keep track of the cards that have been played.

Learning Skills

Provides practice in:

• adding • categorizing • keeping several variables in mind • counting in groups (as score is tallied) • visual alertness • calculating probabilities • memory • reasoning ability (especially ability to judge wisest course among several alternatives)

New words: "names trump"

Cards. Thirty-two card deck: Ace, King, Queen, Jack, 10 down to 7 in each suit.

Rank of cards. 10 (high), Ace, King, Queen, Jack, 9, 8, 7 in each suit.

Point count of cards. 10 = 5 points, Ace = 4 points, King = 3 points, Queen = 2 points, Jack = 1 point.

The object of the game. To earn points by taking in tricks containing valuable cards.

First of all. Dealer lays out two rows of 4 cards face down on the table, a row in front of each player. Eight cards then are dealt to each player, and a card is faced up on each of the eight layout cards. Usual order of dealing is eight face-down layout cards, then three cards are dealt at a time to each player; next eight face-up cards on the table, then two cards at a time to each player; and then three at a time to each.

Play. Dealer chooses the trump suit, and the opponent leads *any card*. Players may play cards from their hand or from the face-up cards on their side of the table. Each player must follow suit if he can; otherwise he must trump or play any other card. He must take a trick in if he can. The player who takes in a trick leads to the next trick.

When a face-up card from the table is played, the one beneath it is turned over. However, the player who leads a card from the table may wait until his opponent has played before exposing the bottom card.

DOUGHNUT

Ages: 7 to adult
Players: 2 to 5

This is a fairly simple introduction to games with trump, and to the art of trying to win tricks.

Learning Skills

Players practice:
● categorizing ● counting ● subtracting and adding ● judging cardinal value of numbers

---

Rank of cards. Ace (high), King, Queen, Jack, 10 down to 2 (low).

First of all. Each player is credited with 20 points. Five cards are dealt to each player. The next card is turned up in the center of the table to indicate the trump suit.

The object of the game. To win as many tricks as possible by playing the highest ranking card of the suit led or a trump card.

Play. First player leads any card. Other players must follow suit, or, if they cannot, must play a trump card or discard. Player of the highest card of the suit led, or of the highest trump takes in the trick. The player who takes in the trick plays first on the next trick.

Scoring. At the end of each hand, a point is deducted from the player's score for every trick taken in. If a player takes in no tricks 5 points are *added* to his score. Cards are shuffled, deal passes to the left for a new hand. Play continues until one player's score reaches 0, and he is declared winner.

OH HELL!

This is an ideal game to introduce children to bidding. This is not to be confused with another game named "Oh Hell" by a little boy who, in describing it, told his mother, "They call out numbers, and one person says 'Bingo!' and everybody else says 'Oh Hell!' "

At the first deal with only one card in the hand, the bidder has two possibilities, 0 or 1; and it is easy for the beginner to consider the likelihood of one or the other alternative, then work up gradually to more complex considerations.

Learning Skills

Players practice:

• categorizing • counting • judging cardinal value of numbers • calculating probabilities • developing strategies • modifying goals; adapting to external demand

---

Rank of cards. Ace, King, Queen, Jack, 10 down to 2 (low).

First of all. The game consists of a series of deals. In the first hand, the dealer deals one card to each player, turns the next card over on top of the deck for trump, and players bid and play.

At the next hand, the deal passes to the next player and 2 cards are dealt to each player; then at each subsequent deal, 3, 4, 5, 6 and so on up to 15 cards (for two or three players), up to 13 cards for four players; and 10 for five players. When, on the thirteenth deal for four players, there is no remaining card to turn over, the game is played in no trump.

Bidding. Beginning at the dealer's left, each player in turn bids the number of tricks he thinks he can take. This is recorded by the scorekeeper.

The object of the game. To win the exact number of tricks bid.

Play. First player plays any card he chooses. Other players must follow suit. If they cannot they may play a trump or discard. Trick is taken in by player of the highest card (the highest trump if trumps have been played, or the highest card of the suit led, if there are no trumps played). Winner of a trick leads to the next trick.

Scoring. If a player gets more or fewer tricks than he bid, his score for that hand is zero (nothing).

If he makes his bid exactly he gets 10 points plus the number of tricks he took in. If he bid zero, and took in no tricks, he gets 10 points plus the total number of tricks in that hand.

At the end of the prescribed number of deals (determined by the number of players—see above), the scores are totalled, and the player with the highest score is the winner.

Comments. Skillful play consists in developing strategies not only for winning tricks, but also for losing tricks where it is necessary not to exceed the tricks bid.

Once in a while a moralistic youngster is shocked by the name of the game, and says, "That's a bad word." I use the occasion for a little moralizing of my own and explain that there are no "bad words." There are words that hurt people's feelings, words that offend some people because of their associations, and words that social convention have made taboo. We talk about how some conventions can be relaxed among good friends, about the origins of taboos, about the origins of other so called bad words, thus the card game has led us into a bit of geography, history, sociology, linguistics, and maybe even psychotherapy.

CASINO

Luck, memory, logic, mathematical skill, alertness interact to make this an entertaining game.

Learning Skills

Provides practice in:

    ● matching ● adding ● keeping track of several variables

      New words: take in, hold, build, combine

Rank of cards. Cards have no rank, but their numerical value is considered. Aces = 1, two = 2, etc. Jack, Queen, King have no numerical value.

Special point value is given to each Ace; to 10 of diamonds (the Good Ten or *Big Casino*); and to the 2 of spades (*Little Casino*).

First of all. Four cards are dealt to each player, and 4 cards face up on the table, usually dealt two at a time in rotation. After these are played out, four cards are dealt again to the players, but no more to the table. After each set of four cards is played out, four new ones are dealt out to each player until the deck is used up.

The object of the game. To earn the highest number of points by taking in: ● the greatest number of cards: 3 points ● the greatest number of spades: 1 point ● the 10 of diamonds: 2 points ● the 2 of spades: 1 point ● Aces, each worth: 1 point ● all the cards on the table in one play (a Sweep): 1 point.

Play. Play begins at the dealer's left, and first player may do one of the following:

(1) Match: Play a card of the same denomination as one on the table, and take both in (e.g., if there is a Queen on the table, and player has a Queen in his hand he puts the two together face down in front of him to count toward his point score.)

(2) Combine: He may combine two cards on the table to equal the numerical value of one he has in his hand, and take them in with the card in his hand. If, for example, there are a 5 and 2 on the table, he may take them in with a 7 from his hand. He may also take in several combinations with the same total (e.g., a 5 and a 2, and a 4 and a 3).

(3) Hold: He may play a card of the same denomination as one on the table, directly onto its match, (or to a combination that equals it in numerical value), and say "holding [naming the cards] " (e.g., "holding tens"). This means that he has another of that denomination in his hand, and plans to take in those cards on a subsequent turn.

(4) Build: He may combine a card or cards on the table with one in his hand to total another card in his hand. For example, if there are a 7 and 2 on the table, the player may put them together, add an Ace from his hand, and say, "Building 10." This means he has a 10 in his hand and plans to take in the cards on a subsequent turn.

(5) If he cannot match, hold, combine or build, he plays a card face up on the table. Next player may do any of the above things as well as: (1) Take in any combination his opponent is holding or building, if he has the card. (2) Build on opponent's "build," e.g., if opponent is building 6 (e.g., with two 3s), player may add a 4 and say "building 10" (providing, of course, he has a 10 in his hand).

A stack that is being "held" (i.e., where a card is matched, or a combination has been made more than once) cannot be built upon.

If there are four players playing partners, a player may add to his partner's "hold" without having another card of that denomination in his hand, e.g., if first player has combined a 4 and a 3, and played a 7 on it, saying "holding 7s," his partner may add a 7 to the stack when his turn comes; or combine a 2 from his hand with a 5 on the table, saying "7s" and add it to the stack, to be taken in by his partner.

When a player's turn comes round again he may raise his own build if he has the appropriate cards. He does not have to take in his "hold" or his "build" at once, providing he can match, take in another combination, capture another player's build or hold, or make another build or hold himself.

If a player takes in all the cards on the table he gets a point for a Sweep. Players can keep track of Sweeps by turning the last card face up when it is placed in the player's stack.

In the final deal of a deck, the player to take in the last match or combination or build, takes in all the remaining cards, but this is not counted as a Sweep.

Comments. Skillful players keep track of cards played and are alert to all possible combinations they may exploit. Also, they look for ways to take in spades and take in many cards at one time. A skillful player may forego taking in cards in order to aim for a more profitable play—the opportunity to take in some point-counting cards, or to be the one to take in all the cards on the table, or make the last "take in."

A HUNDRED & ONE

This is a version of *Casino*, played exactly the same way. Only the numerical value of the cards differ. All number cards are equal to their point value, but aces count 11, as well as 1; Jacks = 12; Queens = 13; and Kings = 14. The winner is the first to reach a score of 101.

Variation. School-age children sometimes vary *Casino* or *101*, by permitting subtraction as well as addition, for combining or building. For example, if there are a 5 and a 3 on the table, a player may say "5 – 3 = 2," and take it in with a 2 from his hand. More complex plays can be made with adding *and* subtracting. For example, if there are a 10, a 4 and a King on the table, a player may say "14 – 10 + 4 = 8," and take them all in with an 8 from his hand. This version not only provides practice in computation, but demands great ingenuity from the players as they perform arithmetical gymnastics in order to be able to take in key cards, or make a Sweep.

A really sophisticated version permits multiplication and division as well. Thus if there were a 10, a 5, and a 2 on the table, a player might say "2 X 10 = 20 ÷ 5 = 4," and take the cards in with a 4.

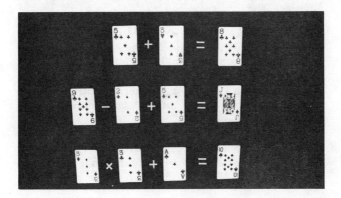

SWEET SIXTEEN

This game was invented by my daughter, Jill (sixteen at the time) to give practice in adding to a youngster she was tutoring in arithmetic. It has turned out to be popular as well as practical.

Learning Skills

Provides practice in:
- adding • learning number combinations up to 16

Value of cards. Jack = 11, Queen = 12, King = 13. All other cards are equal to their face value.

First of all. Deal seven cards to each player. Leave the rest of the cards face-down in the center for a stock pile.

The object of the game. To take in tricks by being the one to play the card that brings the total point value of cards already played to 16.

Play. The first player plays any card from his hand, face-up next to the stock pile, calling out the value of the card (if he plays a 10, he says, "ten"). The other player plays his card on the first one, adding its value to the first. (If he plays a 3 on the 10, he says, "thirteen.") The player who plays the card making the total 16 takes in the trick and leads for the next one.

If a player cannot play a card from his hand without going over 16, he must pick from the stock pile until he can play. The first player to get rid of all his cards is the winner.

TOUGH BEANS

Ages: 6 to adult
Players: 2 to 5

Cards. Full deck of 52.

Value of cards. Each card is counted for its face value: Jacks = 11; Queens = 12; Kings = 13.

The object of the game. To be first to get rid of your cards.

Deal. Eight cards are dealt to each player.

Then. Pack is placed in the middle as a stock and the top card is turned face-up.

Play. Player to the dealer's left plays face-up any card overlapping the turned up card so that the denominations of both are visible. Next player must put down any number of cards whose total denominational value is equal to the *sum* or the *difference* of the two face up cards. For example, if the face-up cards are King and 9, the next player must play cards totalling 22 (sum) or 4 (difference). After showing players his cards, he stacks them so that only one card is visible, and lays them on the face-up cards, again overlapping so there are again two cards (the last one

played by the previous player, and the top card played by the player who has just completed his play) whose sum or difference must be arrived at by the next player.

When a player cannot arrive at the necessary total from the cards in his hand he must draw from the stock until he is able to do so.

TWENTY-NINE

Ages: 7 to adult
Players: 4 (partners)

In this game only the numerical value of the card is considered in play.

Learning Skills

Good game for:

    • practicing adding • learning number combinations up to 29 • socialization • stimulating mental alertness and memory

---

Value of cards. Ace, King, Queen, Jack—each count as one; all other cards are equal to their face value.

First of all. Players cut for partners; and partners sit across from each other. The entire deck is dealt out, one at a time, to each player in turn. Players hold their cards fan-shaped, and group them according to number.

The object of the game. To take in tricks by being the one to play the card that brings the total point value of cards already played to 29.

Play. First player plays a card (e.g., a 10, calling out its total: "ten"). Second player plays a card (say, a 3), announcing the total "13." Third player might play a 9, and

130

says "22." If the fourth player has a 7, he plays it calling "29," and takes in the trick. (The 29 will not always be reached by the fourth card. It may be reached by the third or more often the fifth or sixth.) Player left of the one taking the trick leads to the next trick.

Each player tries to be the one to reach the total of 29, or to play cards that will assist his partner in playing the final card.

The play continues until the cards are all played, or until a player cannot play without going over the total of 29, at which point the game ends. The team with the most tricks is the winning team.

Comments. The winning skills include the ability to keep track of cards played and guess the likelihood of other players having low or high cards. A good player who cannot reach 29 himself will try to play a card low enough to prevent the opponent to his left from reaching 29, but that might enable his partner to play the final card.

BLACK JACK

Ages: 6 to adult
Players: any number

Also called "twenty-one" this is a game played in casinos all over the world by serious gamblers. Nevertheless, it has a place in a list of card games for children, not only because kids love it, but because it is a painless way to practice mental arithmetic, and to begin to think about probabilities.

The serious gamblers have serious rules, with complicated variations, which I am going to omit. The children I play with have taught me a straight-forward game. This is the one I am passing on, because I know it is playable—by some children as young as six. In fact, I have watched children, who did not know any number combinations by heart, find their totals by counting up all the pips on all the cards; or by counting on, starting with, say 10 for a face card, and saying to themselves "11 - 12 - 13 - 14 . . . ," as they point to each of the diamonds in turn on the 7 of diamonds to be added to it.

Learning Skills

Playing the game helps:
• teach number combinations up to 21 • stimulate memory • develop notions of probability

---

Equipment. Deck of 52 cards and plastic chips or counters.

Card values. Jack, Queen, King each count as 10; 2 to 10 each counts its own face value, Ace counts as 1 or 11.

First of all. Cards are dealt face up around, and the first player receiving an Ace becomes dealer and banker. Thereafter deal passes to the left.

Players begin with an equal number of counters. These are used to bet against the dealer (i.e., to bet that one's own hand will be closer to 21 than the dealer's). A maximum bet is decided on by all the players in advance. Before the deal, all players except the dealer place their bets (e.g., 1, 2 or 3 chips).

The object of the game. To get cards totalling 21, or as close to 21 as possible, and to obtain a total greater than the dealer without exceeding 21. Each player in the game plays and bets against the dealer.

Deal. The dealer gives each player including himself one card face up and one face down, one at a time in rotation to the left.

Play. Each player checks his cards for "Blackjack," which consists of an Ace and a 10-point value card, totalling 21. If the dealer has Blackjack, each player, unless he too, has Blackjack, must give the dealer twice the amount he has bet. If a player has Blackjack, and the dealer does not, he collects twice his bet from the dealer. If a player and the dealer both have Blackjack it is a tie, and the dealer wins.

If the dealer does not have Blackjack, and after all players' Blackjacks have been paid off, the other players may "draw." Each player in turn may ask for cards in order to bring his total as close to 21 as possible. He asks for one card at a time (the conventional request is "hit me") until he is satisfied to "stand pat" or stay with the cards he has. Should he go over 21 ("bust") he immediately shows his cards and pays his bet to the dealer. After all the players have drawn cards, or overdrawn, the dealer then faces up his two cards, and draws if he wants to.

Settlement. If the dealer goes over 21, he pays each player who has not overdrawn the amount of his bet. If the dealer

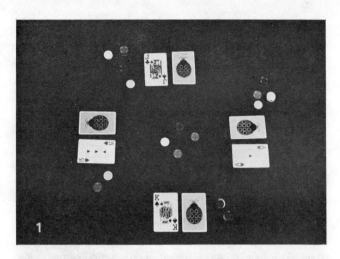

134

has 21 or less, players having the same number are tied, and lose. Players having less than the dealer pay their bet to him. Players closer to 21 than the Dealer win the amount of their bet from him.

Comments. Should a teenager become very intrigued with this game and want to know more about strategies for winning, he would do well to consult Edward C. Thorp's *Beat the Dealer* (Blaisdell Publishing Co., New York, 1962). This fascinating book written by a mathematics professor details an approach to winning at Blackjack based on the mathematical theory of probability. It would be a good book to suggest to a reluctant teen-age reader, with an interest in cards and mathematics. He might even be intrigued enough to report on it to the class.

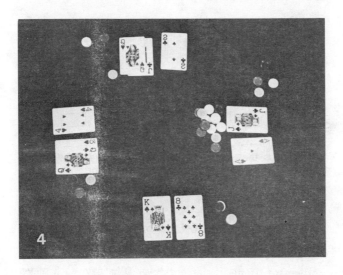

MACAO

Ages: 6 to adult
Players: 2 to 10

This is a variation of *Black Jack* and actually makes a good introduction to the former for children who are just developing their ability to add.

Equipment. Deck of 52 cards and counters.

Card values. Aces count 1; 2 to 9 are equal to their face value; 10, Jack, Queen, King have no point value.

Preliminaries are about the same as in Black Jack.

First of all. Same as *Black Jack*, see previous game.

The object of the game. To get cards totalling 9, or as close to 9 as possible; and to obtain a total greater than the dealer without exceeding 9. Each player bets against the dealer.

Deal. The dealer gives each player including himself one card face down.

Play. Each player checks his card for a "natural" (9, 8 or 7). A 9 entitles him to collect three times his bet; an 8 gets twice his bet; and a 7 the amount of his bet.

If the dealer has a "natural," and a player does not, the player pays the dealer his bet. If both have naturals, the highest card collects. If both have the same natural it is considered a tie, and no payments are made.

If the dealer does not have a natural and after all player's naturals have been paid off, the other players may "draw" as in Black Jack.

Settlement. If the dealer goes over 9 he pays each player who has not overdrawn the amount of his bet.

If the dealer has 9 or less, players having the same number are tied and neither win nor lose. Players having more than the dealer, but 9 or less, win the amount of their bet from the dealer.

FIVE HUNDRED RUMMY

Ages: 7 to adult
Players: 2 to 4

There are dozens of variations of *Rummy*. Although *Gin Rummy* and *Canasta* are more popular with adults, I am listing only my own favorite for play with children. When I was nine years old I learned to add quickly and accurately from counting of points in endless games of *"500."* I've given dozens of other children the same opportunity. Once one *Rummy* game has been learned, others are easily mastered. Consult your official rule book.

Learning Skills

Good game for:
* developing awareness of sets • developing awareness of sequence • practicing visual scanning • practicing adding, and multiplying
New words: meld, run, discard

Cards. Full deck of 52 cards.

Value of cards. Each card is worth its face value except for Ace, which is worth 1 or 15, depending on how it is used. Face cards (Jack, Queen, King) are each worth ten points.

First of all. Deal seven cards to each player. Leave the rest of the deck in the middle as a stock. Turn up the top card of the stock, and put it beside the pile.

The object of the game. To gain points by collecting sets of three or more cards and "melding" them (putting them face up on the table in front of him). Sets may be "three of a kind" (at least three cards of the same face value, e.g., three Kings; three 3s, etc.) or runs—at least three cards of the same suit in sequence, e.g., 3 of diamonds, 4 of diamonds, and 5 of diamonds; or Jack of hearts, Queen of hearts and King of hearts. Ace may be used as both high and low. Sequences of Ace, 2, 3, and Queen King, Ace are both permissible. (King, Ace, 2 is not.)

If players agree, game can be played with "deuces wild." A player holding a 2 may designate it as any card. Thus he can put down two Jacks and a 2 as a set of Jacks; 8 of diamonds, 9 of diamonds, 2 of hearts, as a run. Each players' face-up melds count to his score.

Play. Each player must draw a card from the stock, and discard (play a card to the face-up pile) at each turn.

First player to dealer's left may take the face-up card, providing he can use it immediately to meld (play a set of cards to the table). If he cannot use it, he draws the top card of the stock, and plays a card from his hand to the face-up pile, overlapping it, so that all face up cards are visible.

Subsequent players may take any card from the face-up pile if they can use it as part of a meld, but must take as well all cards that overlap it (cover it).

During a player's turn, before he discards, he may meld any sets he has in his hand, or cards that go with sets already on the table either his own or his opponents'. Thus, if a player or one of his opponents has three Kings face-up on the

138

table, he can put a King from his hand, (and is later credited with ten points). If he, or his opponent, has a run of 7 of clubs, 8 of clubs, 9 of clubs, he can put down a 6 of clubs from his own hand into his own array of melds. Another player may subsequently expand the run with the 5 of clubs. Play continues till one player "goes out." A player may "go out" by melding all of his cards but one, and discarding the final card.

The player who goes out first collects all the cards remaining in the other players' hands and adds them to his score.

Scoring. Each player's score is the total value of cards he has melded (plus the cards a player has collected by "going out"). An Ace in a run of Ace, 2, 3 is counted as 1; in a run of Queen, King, Ace is counted as 15. In a set of 3 Aces, each is worth 15 points. An Ace won from another player's hand by going out is worth 15. After each hand cards are shuffled and redealt. The game continues until one player's score reaches 500.

Strategies. Players must weigh the advantage of taking a large number of cards on the face-up pile in order to get one they want for a meld. Might there be other potentially useful cards there for the player? Is it late in the game, and might he be stuck with many cards in his hand if another player goes out?

Comments. The totalling of points after each hand is superb arithmetic drill. Children quickly learn to multiply 3s to get the value of their sets of three of a kind, and to recognize that the total of a run of three is three times the value of the middle number (thus $6, 7, 8 = 3 \times 7 = 21$); when there are many cards to be totalled, some skillful computers first collect combinations totalling ten, and count by tens. Very little adult intervention is necessary to help them develop the mathematical short cuts. The inherent repetition in playing the game helps them to become effortless and automatic.

SOLITAIRE

Solitaire or *Patience* games are usually played alone, and the player tries, from a variety of initial layouts, to get all the cards in a specified order. Adults are intrigued by the unpredictable movements of the cards and spurred on by the always present, never certain chance of success. It is not only the fascinating antics of the cards that produce the intense involvement of some children in playing *Solitaire*, but the feeling that Destiny is communicating with them through the cards. "If it works out, it means I'm going to get to go to the movies tomorrow," said one youngster as he dealt out the cards; and then, a few minutes later, he added the proviso, "If it works out once in three times." Like the horoscopes in the daily papers, the forecasts are immediately forgotten so it takes years for the faith to diminish.

After parents and teachers have happily watched their youngsters learn to enjoy conversation with adults and play with their peers, they are then eager to make sure these same youngsters learn to enjoy the pleasures of being alone. It is highly desirable for them to find ways of amusing themselves, so that when there are no other children around, the parent does not have always to respond to the cry of, "What shall I do?" and can himself enjoy the pleasures of being alone now and then.

In most families, and most classrooms, not just any kind of self-amusement will do. Indoors, gross physical activities are usually to be discouraged, at least some of the time. So are the outstandingly noisy diversions, the frankly destructive, the very expensive—all spontaneously chosen by many otherwise charming children. Fortunately most children learn to read, or do some kind of handicrafts, or discover the appeal of crossword puzzles, or jigsaw puzzles, and can then pass some time cheerfully, quietly, and constructively. But what of children with learning disabilities, some of whom never reach the point of reading for pleasure, or have learned to regard jigsaw puzzles and crossword puzzles as something to help them with their perceptual problems and their spelling difficulties, but never recreational. For this group, *Solitaire* might be a real boon, as well as the pleasant diversion it is for others. Learning and playing most of the games require no great skill, although in some there are clever strategies to be cultivated. In every game, though, there is the unique form imposed by the rules and the fascination of the movements of the cards.

KLONDIKE

When some people refer to *Solitaire*, they mean this particular game, probably the most popular of all solitaires.

Learning Skills

The game provides practice in:

 • counting • numerical sequence • categorizing • maintaining visual alertness • visual and auditory rhythms • left to right organization

---

Layout. Counting aloud, while dealing the layout helps some children get the rhythm of it. Do it like this: Count and deal out seven cards in a row—the first, face up; the next six face down. Then, starting to the right of the face-up card, begin the count and deal again (this time from one to six), covering up the other cards, facing up the card that accompanies the count of one, and facing down the others. Continue in this way, always starting to the right of the last faced-up card; facing up the card that accompanies

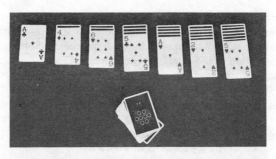

the count of one, and each time counting one less than the time before. When the last card is faced up, there will be 28 cards in seven piles, the one furthest to the left consisting of only one face-up card, the next of one face-down card, covered by one face-up; the next with two face-down, covered by one face-up, and so on until the last pile on the right with six face-down and one face-up.

The rest of the deck is used as a stock. In play, Aces are released and placed above the layout as a foundation.

The object of the game. To build on all foundation Aces in upward sequence, according to suit, until the King is reached.

Play. Aces from the layout are put in the foundation row. Cards exposed on the layout are built on in downward sequence, in alternating color. (On a red 9, black 8 may be placed, then a red 7, and so on). If a card from the layout is moved, the card below is faced-up and becomes available for play.

The stock is held face down and cards are taken three at a time from the top, and faced-up. The top faced-up card can be used in play—to build on the foundation Aces, or to build downward in alternating colors on the layout. Any time a card from the layout, or stock, is used in play, the card below it becomes available. Available spaces in the layout are filled with Kings, or with sequences that start with Kings. Any sequence may be moved in its entirety if there is a suitable spot for the card that heads it.

When the stock has been dealt out, it is turned over, without shuffling, and run through, three at a time, as before. This is repeated until there are no more possible plays, or until the game is won.

FIRING SQUAD

Learning Skills

Provides practice in:

• recognizing quantitative value of numbers • developing idea of higher and lower • categorizing • visual scanning

New words: column, top (card farthest away from player; i.e., first card in the column)

Initial layout. Face up four cards in a row at the top of the table or on the floor, sufficiently far away from the player to permit him to lay out the rows from there toward him.

The object of the game. To end up with one row only, consisting of the four Aces.

Play. If any of the cards in the horizontal row are of the same suit, remove the cards lower in rank to the trash pile, leaving only the highest card of each suit, each in its original position.

Then deal, in a horizontal row left to right, four more cards immediately below the first row. Repeat the elimination process; that is, remove cards lower in rank than cards of the same suit in that row, as before. When the lower denomination card is removed from the bottom row, take the card at the top of the *vertical* column in which that card came and place it at the bottom.

Continue to play rows of four cards until the deck is used up or the game is won.

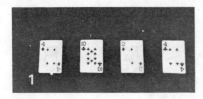
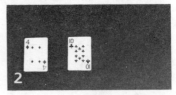

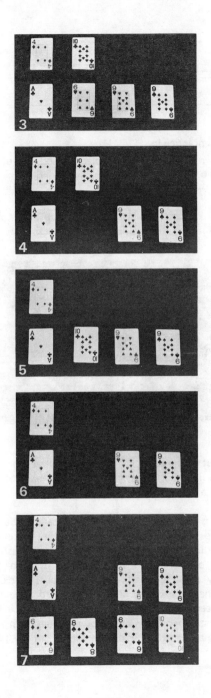

145

THREES IN A CORNER

Learning Skills

Provides practice in:
   ● numerical sequence (both up and down) ● categorizing ● counting ● maintaining a variable set

Layout. Five cards are dealt out face up in the form of a cross. The rest of the deck is used as a stock.

The object of the game. To get all four threes in the corners and build on them, in upward sequence, cards of their own suit, until a two is reached in each suit.

Play. Cards from the stock are turned up one at a time, and used if possible on the layout, or in the corners. If they cannot be used they are placed face up on a Trash Pile. The top card of the Trash Pile may be used in play if a possibility presents itself. On the layout, cards are built from highest card (the 2) in downward sequence, Ace, King, Queen, Jack, 10, 9, 8, 7, 6, 5, to 4 (low) without regard to suit or color. Cards may be taken from the layout to add to a sequence. Spaces in the layout are filled from

the stock. 3s from the layout or from the stock are put into the corners of the cross, and are built on in upward sequence according to suit—ending always with a 2. The stock may be used only once.

ACCORDION

This is a compelling exercise. Although the game is not often won it is hard to stop trying. I have seen children go on week-long jags of playing this game over and over, fascinated by the accordion-like properties of the rows of cards.

Learning Skills

Playing helps practice:

    ● visual alertness ● the ability to maintain a variable set ● visual scanning ● matching ● categorizing ● counting

---

Although mainly a game of chance, there are often opportunities to choose the most profitable of two plays that appear simultaneously. The player must be alert to all possibilities that present themselves.

The object of the game. To try to get all the cards on one pile.

Play. Cards are dealt out, one at a time, in a horizontal row. A card may be placed on the card immediately to its left, or on the third card to its left (jumping over two piles), if it is of the same suit or same denomination. Similarly, entire piles can be moved to the left (to the adjacent pile, or to the pile reached by jumping over two) if the top cards are of the same denomination or same suit.

BETROTHAL

Like *Accordion*, this game is fascinating. Little skill is demanded, but there are occasionally opportunities to choose the better of two possible plays. This requires the player to be alert, and to be able to think ahead to the consequences of a given play.

Learning Skills

Playing gives practice in:

- visual alertness ● visual scanning ● matching ● categorizing ● counting ● maintaining a variable set

---

Preliminaries. The Queen of hearts is put on the top of the deck, so it is the first card played, and the King of hearts is put on the bottom so it is the last card played.

The object of the game. To get the Queen and King of hearts side by side.

Play. Cards are dealt out, one at a time, in a horizontal row. When a card is dealt that is of the same denomination, or the same suit, as the second card to its left, the card between them may be removed and put aside. Whenever a card matches, in suit or denomination, the third card to its left, the two intervening cards may be removed.

SPACES

This takes a long time to play, and a big table, or big chunk of floor space to play it on.

Learning Skills

Provides practice in:
- left-right orientation • visual scanning • sequencing

Layout. Cards are dealt out face up into four rows of 13 each.

The object of the game. To try to get four rows of cards in suit sequences from 2 to King.

Play. The four Aces are removed from the layout and put aside. Each space left by an Ace is filled by a card one higher and of the same suit as the card to the left of the space. Thus, if a space follows a 4 of spades, the layout is scanned for the 5 of spades, which is put in the space. The new spaces are filled in the same way. A space to the right of a King cannot be filled. A space at the extreme left of each row is to be filled by any 2. The 2 determines the suit sequence of that row, and must not be moved after being placed.

When there are no more possibilities for play (that is, when all spaces are to the right of Kings), then all cards not correctly placed (i.e., in suit sequence from 2) are taken up with the four Aces, reshuffled, and dealt again, filling in the gaps left on the layout. Again Aces are removed and the play resumes.

It is permissible to pick up the cards, reshuffle, and deal them out three times altogether. If the sequences are not complete after that the game is lost.

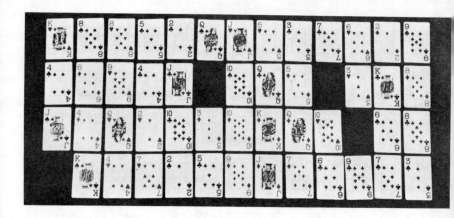

TRAIN SOLITAIRE

As the title suggests, this game earned its popularity on trains where there was no space available for a layout. It has helped ward-off restlessness or boredom for my children on car trips and in crowded waiting rooms.

Learning Skills

Provides practice in:
   ● visual alertness ● matching ● categorizing ● keeping several variables in mind ● counting

---

The object of the game. To try to be left with fewer than five cards.

Play. The deck is held in one hand, face down. Four cards are faced up from the bottom of the deck and fanned out on top of the pack. If the first and fourth cards are of the same suit the two cards in between are discarded. If the first and fourth cards are of the same denomination all four cards are removed. If the first and fourth cards are adjacent, cards of the same suit, the top three are removed. Cards are faced up again from the bottom so that there are always four playing cards. If none of the four cards can be dis-

carded another card is faced up from the bottom, but only the top four faced up cards are used in play. Play continues until the deck is used up and no more discards can be made. Remaining cards can be turned over so that play can be resumed. This is allowed only once.

MORE SOLITAIRES

The following solitaires all provide practice in addition. Number combinations are rehearsed over and over again until they are memorized. These are good exercises for pupils in an arithmetic class. The teacher might ask a youngster who has finished his assignment to get a deck of cards and play any one of the following solitaires. To solve the problem of adequate feedback (how does the child know if he has made a mistake in addition?), introduce him to an age-old tradition in card playing—the "kibbitzer." Another child is assigned to look over the shoulder of the player. The sole function of the kibbitzer is to spot any errors in play, and point them out.

ELEVENS (A)

Value of cards. Number cards are equal to their face value; Jacks, Queens, Kings have no value.

Layout. Twelve cards in three rows of four each, face up. The rest of the deck is used as a stock.

The object of the game. To cover all the layout piles with face cards, Jacks on the first row, Queens on the second row, Kings on the third row.

Play. Use cards from the stock to cover any two cards that total eleven. As Jacks, Queens, and Kings turn up, put them on the bottom of the deck, so that the last cards in play are the face cards.

TENS

Value of cards. Number cards equal their face value. Jacks, Queens, Kings have no value.

Layout. Deal out 13 cards face up in a horizontal row. The rest of the deck becomes a stock.

The object of the game. To discard all the cards.

Play. Discard any two cards that total ten. Discard 10, Jack, Queen, King together when all four are available in one suit. Fill spaces in layout from stock and continue to play until all the cards are discarded, or there are no further plays.

TEN, TWENTY, THIRTY

Value of cards. Number cards are equal to their face value; Jacks, Queens, Kings are each equal to ten.

Layout. Deal out cards in a row one at a time.

The object of the game. To discard all of the cards but one.

Play. As the cards are being dealt remove any three adjacent cards that total 10, 20 or 30. Thus, an Ace, 9, and King side by side could be discarded. So could 5, 3, 2; or Jack, 10, Queen.

THIRTEEN

Value of Cards. Number cards are equal to their face value; Jacks = 11; Queens = 12; Kings = 13.

Layout. Deal out 10 cards in two rows of five. The rest of the deck is used as a stock.

The object of the game. To get rid of all the cards.

Play. Discard any two cards that total 13. Remove Kings by themselves. Fill spaces in layout from the stock. Continue playing until all the cards are used up or until there are no more possible plays.

ELEVENS (B)

Value of cards. Number cards are equal to their face value. Jacks, Queens, Kings have no value.

Layout. Deal out nine cards in three rows of three. The rest of the deck is a stock.

The object of the game. To remove all the cards.

Play. Remove any two cards that total 11. Remove Jacks, Queens, and Kings in trios of one of each, regardless of suits. Fill spaces in the layout from the stock. Continue playing until all the cards are discarded, or until there are no more possible plays.

FIFTEENS

Value of cards. Number cards (1 to 9) are equal to their face value. Ten, Jack, Queen, King have no numerical value.

Layout. Deal out 16 cards in four rows of four. The rest of the deck becomes the stock.

The object of the game. To remove all the cards.

Play. Discard any two cards that total 15. Discard 10s, Jacks, Queens, Kings in quartets of one suit. Fill in spaces in the layout from the stock. Continue playing until all the cards are discarded, or until there are no more possible plays.

FOURTEEN

Value of cards. Number cards are equal to their face value. Jack = 11; Queen = 12; King = 13.

Layout. Deal out the entire deck into 12 face-up piles, counting out a row of 12, and then covering each one with one card, and then again, until the deck is used up. This will give five cards in each of the first four piles, and four cards in each of the remaining eight. The top cards are available for play.

The object of the game. To remove all the cards.

Play. Remove any two cards that total 14.

PYRAMID (13)

Value of cards. Number cards are equal to their face value. Jack = 11; Queen = 12; King = 13.

Layout. Deal out a pyramid-like arrangement of 28 cards, the first row with one card, the next with two overlapping that one, the third with three overlapping the two of the previous row, and so on. The last row will consist of seven cards. The rest of the deck is used as the stock.

The object of the game. To get rid of all the cards in the layout, the stock and the Trash Pile.

Play. Remove and put aside any two cards on the layout that total 13, or any single King, as long as no cards overlap them. Then turn up cards from the stock one at a time. If they can be combined with available cards from the layout to total 13, discard them. If not, lay them face up on a Trash Pile. The top card of the Trash Pile can be used in play, combined either with a card from the stock, or with a card from the layout.

Continue playing until all cards—from layout, stock and Trash Pile have been removed; or until there are no further plays.

DOUBLES

(Called also, *Casting Out Thirteens*.) This game provides practice in multiplying (doubling) and subtraction.

Cards. Full deck of 52 cards.

Value of cards. Number cards are equal to their face value; Jacks = 11; Queens = 12; Kings have no value.

Layout. Deal a row of seven face-up cards. If there are any Kings in the row place them on the bottom of the deck and replace them. Place one face-up card below as a foundation card. The rest of the deck is placed face down as the hand or stock pile.

The object of the game. To play out all the cards except the four Kings on the foundation by playing each time the card that is double the face value of the one on top of the foundation. Whenever the double value is greater than thirteen, thirteen is subtracted. Thus on a 4 play 8; on an 8 play 3 (2 × 8 = 16; 16 − 13 = 3). On a 3, play a 6; on a 6, play a Queen (Queen = 12); on a Queen, play a 9; (2 × 12 = 24; 24 − 13 = Jack) etc.

Play. Any card from the row of seven may be used in a play. If it is placed on the foundation, it is replaced from the hand or Trash Pile. If a King turns up it is left there and is a dead card. Cards from the hand are faced up one at a time, played onto the foundation if possible, or placed face up on a Trash Pile. Only the top card of the Trash Pile may be used in play. When the hand is used up, the Trash Pile may be turned over and dealt out again. Two redeals are allowed altogether.

EVENS

Practice in adding; in recognizing even and odd numbers.

Cards. Deck of 40 (remove all face cards from deck of 52).

The object of the game. To discard the entire deck.

Play. Deal cards one at a time in a horizontal row. Remove any two adjacent cards that add up to an even number.

ODDS

This is played like *Evens* except that two adjacent cards must total an odd number in order to be discarded.

MULTIPLES

This series of games provides practice in adding, multiplying and dividing.

Cards. Deck of 40 (regular deck with all face cards removed.

The object of the game. To discard the entire deck.

Play. Deal cards one at a time in a horizontal row. Remove any number of consecutive cards that add up to a multiple of the number specified. The game may be played as multiples of three, multiples of four, and multiples of five.

Comments. For children who have not yet learned products by heart, have multiplication tables visible so they can check their totals as they go along to see when a total is divisible by (a multiple of) the number specified. Playing the game over and over for fun provides the repetition some children need to help memorize the products.

This solitaire can become a group activity if several children, each with his own deck, play simultaneously. The one with the fewest cards left over at the end of each deal is the winner. The winner can name the key *multiple* for the next game.

GRANDFATHER'S CLOCK

Layout. In clocklike formation lay out the 9 of clubs (where the 12 should be), the 10 of hearts (where the 1 should be), the Jack of spades (in the place of the 2), and continuing around the clock the Queen of diamonds, King of clubs, 2 of hearts, 3 of spades, 4 of diamonds, 5 of clubs,

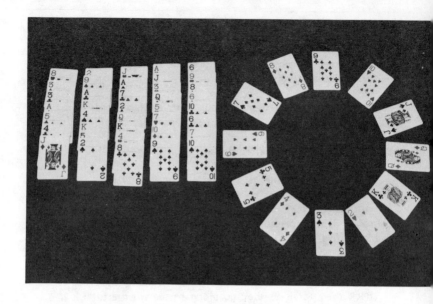

6 of hearts, 7 of spades, 8 of diamonds. These constitute the foundations. They lay out five columns of eight overlapping cards.

The object of the game. To build up on each foundation pile in suits until it reaches the appropriate number of the clock. Jack = 11, Queen = 12. Aces are placed on Kings. Thus on the Queen of diamonds, to reach its clock value, you place in turn the King of diamonds, Ace of diamonds, 2 of diamonds, and 3 of diamonds.

Play. The bottom cards of the column are available for play. They may be built on the foundations or built in downward sequence (suit is not a factor here). Cards may be taken from the bottom of the columns to play on the foundation, or placed in descending order on other bottom cards regardless of suit. If an entire column is played out, any bottom card may be used to fill the space.

158

CLOCK SOLITAIRE

Learning Skills

Playing helps:
  ● develop awareness of numerical sequence ● develop awareness of the position of the numbers of the clock ● practice in visual scanning ● practice in number recognition

Cards. Full deck of 52 cards.

Value of cards. Aces = 1; number cards are equal to their face value; Jack = 11; Queen = 12; King = 13.

The object of the game. To have in each pile all four cards of the same denomination representing the numbers on the clock face, and a pile of 4 kings in the middle.

Layout. Deal cards one at a time into 13 piles face down, arranged with twelve in a circle and one in the middle. The twelve piles in the circle represent the numbers of a clock; twelve at the top, six at the bottom, etc. The pile in the middle, representing the hands is for the King. Turn up the first card from the King pile, and place it, face up under the

159

pile which represents its number, e.g. if it is a Jack, it goes just before the top card in the upper left part of the circle to represent 11. Turn up the top card of the pile to which you have assigned it, and put this card face up under the appropriate pile. Continue this way. If the Kings are all in place, and no further move can be made before all the cards are in place, then the game is lost.

FOUR KINGS

Value of cards. Number cards equal their face value; Jack = 11, Queen = 12; King = 13.

Layout. Two rows of four cards each. The first row: Ace, 2, 3, 4—suits do not matter. The second row: any 2, 4, 6, 8. The second row is the foundation row. The rest of the pack constitutes the Stock.

Play. The stock is turned up one card at a time and cards are played on the bottom row (Foundation Row), when

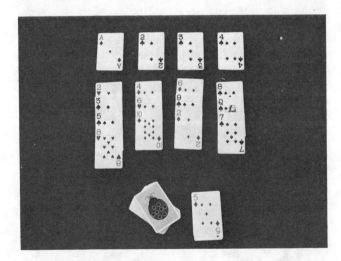

they are equal in value to the exposed card plus the card directly above it. Thus, if a nine is turned up it can go on the 6 because 6 + 3 (above it) = 9. Then a Queen may be placed on the 9 because 9 + 3 (above it) = 12. When the total of a column exceeds 13, subtract 13 from the total to get the card to be played. Thus if there is a Queen in the third space in the bottom row, add 12 + 3 and subtract 13. This means that a 2 is needed to cover the Queen. If a card cannot be played it is put face up on a Trash Pile. The top card of the Trash Pile may be used in play.

When the stock is used up it may be turned over and redealt twice. The game is won if in the three deals the player gets four Kings covering the four foundation cards.

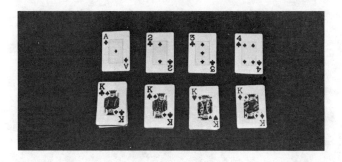

CARD TRICKS

The first cards ever made were probably the Tarot cards, used for divination and prophecy. The association of cards with mystery and magic is an ancient one. Magicians have always included card tricks in their repertoire. Cards are flexible and just the right size for the sleight-of-hand kind of magic—for making cards disappear and reappear, for performing shuffles that are not what they seem to be, for false cuts and fancy fans. Other properties of cards make them ideal for mathematically based tricks: they can be counted, credited with their face value and tallied, and ordered and categorized in a variety of ways.

It seems only fitting that once a youngster is introduced to cards he should be taught how to work magic with them. I recommend that every teacher keep a card trick or two up his sleeve (figuratively speaking, of course), for diversions or bribes (reinforcements for desirable behavior) when the "natives" are restless. I knew one teacher with an enormous repertoire of card tricks who had an elaborate behavior modification scheme going; instead of *m & m*s or tokens as reinforcements, she doled out the secrets to her card tricks to those children who completed their assignments correctly.

I am not going to describe any sleight-of-hand card tricks. I have never learned how to do the tricks dependent on fast-moving, nimble fingers, but there is probably no better way to develop real manual agility than to practice and perfect the art of palming a card or faking a shuffle. However, to learn this kind of prestidigitation you must consult books on magic written by professional magicians.

Here are a few mathematical tricks. A would-be magician will cheerfully memorize rules, rehearse number combinations, work on computation skill as he does these over and over for long-suffering family members in order to master a trick that will dazzle and amaze his friends.

COUNT DOWN I

This trick, either version, gives both audience and performer a chance to practice counting and rapid mental computation.

Equipment. Deck of 52 cards.

First of all. Magician turns his back, or leaves the room, and someone in the audience counts out three stacks of cards as follows: he turns a card face up and begins counting with the number on the card (Ace = 1; Jack = 11; Queen = 12; King = 13). He continues until he reaches 13 (e.g., if he turns up a 7 he adds cards, one at a time counting 8, 9, 10, until he reaches 13). When a stack is completed, he turns it over face-down, and starts a new one.

Trick. Magician returns, counts remaining cards, asks someone to face up the top card of any two of the piles, and then announces the denomination of the top card of the third pile.

Magician's secret. Magician adds the numbers of the faced-up cards; adds to the total 10; then subtracts the new total from the number of remaining cards. The value of the remainder gives the denomination of the top card of the third pile.

For example: Number of left-over cards = 27
    Turned-up cards: Jack, 5
    Step 1: Sum of turned-up cards: $11 + 5 = 16$
    Step 2: Add 10: $16 + 10 = 26$
    Step 3: Left over cards—Sum: $27 - 26 = 1$
    Step 4: Remaining top card is an Ace.

Variation. This variation on the magician's secret was developed by a six-year old who wanted to do the trick, but had not yet learned to add and subtract numbers above 20.

After top cards of two piles were turned up, magician took the remaining cards (cards left over after stacks were made) and counted off separately the number of each of the faced-up cards; then counted out ten cards. Next he counted out the rest of the cards which equalled the face value of the hidden top card.

In the above example, he would have counted off 11 cards, then 5 cards, then 10 cards, and counted the remainder—in this case one card which would mean that the hidden top card was an Ace.

COUNT DOWN II

Equipment. Deck of 52 cards.

First of all. Magician turns his back or leaves the room while a member of the audience deals out the deck into piles as follows: he turns a card face up and begins counting with the number on the card (Ace = 1; Jack, Queen, King are each counted as 10), counting aloud and dealing cards on top of the first one until he reaches 12. If for example, the first card is a King, he counts 10, 11, 12; adding two cards to complete the pile. When a pile is completed it is turned over face down, and a new pile is begun.

All cards are counted out this way until no more piles can be made, because there would not be enough to reach the count of 12.

Trick. Magician returns, counts remaining cards, and after a short period of concentration announces the total of the top cards in the face-down stacks. Audience turns them up and confirms his total.

Magician's secret. Count the piles (e.g., 6)
    Subtract 4 from the total (6 − 4 = 2)
    Multiply remainder by 13 (13 × 2 = 26)
    To this add number of left-over cards (e.g., 5)
    The mystery total 26 + 5 = 31

THE LINE UP

The magician who does this trick gets to practice simple adding, counting, keeping track of a total, and subtracting 10. Members of the audience must count accurately and get to practice left-to-right movements.

Equipment. Ten cards of a suit—Ace through 10.

First of all. Lay the cards face down in a row, in order from 1 to 10. Magician tells the audience that while he is not looking they may move cards one at a time from the left-hand side of the row—as many as they want up to 9. Before turning his back, he moves some himself to demonstrate the procedure.

Trick. Magician turns his back. Some cards are moved. The magician picks up one of the ten cards, and the number on it tells how many cards have been moved. He can do this over and over again.

Magician's secret. On his first trial the magician counts from the right the number of cards he moved during his demonstration. He picks up the next card. Each time he repeats the trick he keeps track of the total number of cards moved so far (his own and the audience's); counts this total from the right, turns over the one after this which gives the number of cards moved on the last trial.

Whenever the total of cards moved reaches ten or more, he subtracts ten, and uses only the remainder.

If he turns up a 10 he knows that no cards have been moved.

BACK TO FRONT

Here is a trick where the magician must practice to develop enough tactile sensitivity in his fingers to count the cards behind his back; and must learn to halve (divide by two) even numbers to 52.

Equipment. An even number of cards—half red and half black. For less dextrous children, or children whose mathematical skills are limited, use only 10 cards.

Trick. The cards of one color are turned face up and put into a packet; the cards of the other color are faced down in a packet. The two packets are thoroughly shuffled together by a spectator. The magician puts the cards behind his back. Then he brings out two packets of cards, one in each hand. The number of face-up cards in each packet is the same; and the face-up cards in each packet are opposite in color.

Magician's secret. When the cards are out of sight behind his back, the magician divides them in half. He must count off exactly half. He then turns over one packet before he brings them out. The trick always works. Older children might like to figure out why.

SPELLING MAGIC

Equipment. Full deck of 52 cards.

Trick. A member of the audience is asked to cut the deck as close to the middle as he can. (This trick won't work unless the cut is very near the middle.) He is to take the half off the top and put it down beside the remaining cards. Then he is instructed to count the cards in the bottom section of the deck. To pick a card, he is to add together the 2 digits of the total he gets, and count up to that figure from the bottom (for example, if he counts 22 cards in the pile, he adds 2 + 2 = 4. Then he looks at and remembers the fourth card from the bottom, leaving it in place. Then, this pile, with the chosen card, is replaced on the other half. The magician starts dealing off the cards from the top, one at a time; putting one down for each letter as he spells aloud, L-E-T T-H-E C-A-R-D A-P-P-E-A-R N-O-W. As he says the last letter he turns over the card which proves to be the chosen card.

Magician's secret. This trick works because if you take any two-digit number, add its digits together, and subtract the results from the original number, the answer will be a multiple of 9. Since we are deliberately using almost half a deck, the original number is likely to be in the twenties. Subtracting the sum of the digits will yield 18. That is, there will be 18 cards in the pack above the one that has been selected. The chosen card will inevitably be 19th from the top. The magician must choose a mystery phrase of exactly 19 letters, and turn over the chosen card as the last letter is spelled. It is advisable to have a number of phrases to choose from, particularly if the trick is ever to be performed more than once for the same audience. Suitable phrases include:

M-A-G-I-C E-N-T-E-R M-Y F-I-N-G-E-R-S
M-Y-S-T-E-R-Y C-A-R-D C-O-M-E T-O M-E
I W-I-L-L C-H-O-O-S-E T-H-I-S C-A-R-D
Y-O-U-R C-A-R-D I-S R-I-G-H-T H-E-R-E

If a teacher has some key words she wants a child to learn to spell she can built a phrase around them. The young magician will practice the trick enough to guarantee that he memorizes their spelling.

ADD IT UP

This trick is a real incentive to repetitive drill in arithmetic. Both adding and subtracting are practiced. Children who like to do this trick work up considerable speed and accuracy in computation. Many like it so much that they do it for fun without an audience, removing a card without looking at it, and testing their ability to figure out the missing card.

Equipment. A deck of 52 cards.

Trick. Magician asks someone in the audience to pick a card from the pack, look at it and hold it. The magician then takes the deck, turns over the cards one at a time, and then names the missing card (denomination only).

Magician's secret. Count cards in the following way:
    Ace = 1
    Number cards = their face value
    Jack = 11
    Queen = 12
    King = 13

Then a full deck totals 364.

By keeping a running total of the cards (as you turn them over), and subtracting the final total from 364, you can figure out the face value of the missing card.

However, unless you are a whiz at computation this method may lead to slip-ups. Even if your total is out by just 1, you cannot name the card correctly. An easier method is the following:

Count Kings as 0, and add nothing to the total when a King turns up. Every time the total exceeds 20 drop 20, and leave only the remainder. For example, if you add two Jacks and get 22, forget the 20, and consider your total so far to be 2. You will end up with a number from 0 to 12. Subtract this from 12 to determine the missing card.

If your total had been 0 then 12 − 0 = 12; and the card you are to name is a Queen. If your total had been 3, then the card is a 9 (12 − 3 = 9).

CALCULATION

Equipment. A deck of 52 cards.

Trick. Magician asks someone in the audience to pick any card from the pack. Then he asks him to perform the following calculations mentally, and announce the result.
    Step 1: Double the face value of the card (Aces count as 1, Jacks = 11, Queens = 12, Kings = 13).
    Step 2: Add 3
    Step 3: Multiply by 5
    Step 4: Add 1 if its a club
                 2 if its a diamond
                 3 if its a heart
                 4 if its a spade

As soon as he hears the result, the magician names the card.

Magician's secret. The magician mentally subtracts 15 from the total. The last digit of the new total represents the suit of the card (1 = club, 2 = diamonds, 3 = hearts, 4 = spades). The left-hand digit or digits represent the denomination. E.g., 74 = 7 of spades; 122 = Queen of clubs.

SPELLING THE CARDS

Equipment. 13 cards of one suit, from Ace to King.

Trick. Magician holds the pack of 13 cards face down in his hand. Then he spells aloud the names of the cards in order removing a card from the top and placing it on the bottom as each letter is spelled. When the spelling of a card is completed, he says its name, at the same time turning the top card up on the table in front of him. It is invariably the card spelled. He proceeds in this way "A-C-E Ace; T-W-O two"; until all the cards are spelled through J-A-C-K Jack; Q-U-E-E-N Queen; K-I-N-G King.

Magician's secret. Before the trick he arranges cards as follows: 3, 8, 7, Ace, Queen, 6, 4, 2, Jack, King, 10, 9, 5.

If he forgets the arrangement he can always reconstruct it by putting down 13 blanks (_ _ _ _ _ _ _ _ _ _ _ _ _), working from left to right, begin to spell the cards, as in the trick, pointing to a blank, as he says each letter. When he comes to the name he writes in the cards; thus the Ace will be in the fourth space and he writes in _ _ _ A _ _ _ 2 _ _ _ _ _; the two will be in the eighth space; he continues this way, skipping over filled spaces until all the blanks are filled. This is the arrangement of the cards.

Variation. The trick is equally mystifying if words other than the names of cards are used and the cards, put down as each word is said, come out in order from Ace to King. The children can choose the 13 words they want to spell out, and derive the set-up arrangements they need in advance.

I have taught youngsters with severe spelling disabilities the months of the year and the days of the week, by introducing them to variations on this trick. In practicing the trick they managed for the first time to memorize the names, the order and the spellings. In one version we made the words to be spelled January, February, March, April, May, June, July, August, September, October, November, December and as they were spelled the cards arranged themselves from Ace to King. The arrangement was of course 5, 9, Q, 7, 2, 10, 4, A, 6, 8, J, 3. In another version, we used only seven cards (Ace to 7 in one suit) and spelled the days of the week. The appropriate arrangement is 2, 6, 7, 3, 5, 4, A, (starting with Sunday—the first day of the week.)

COMBINATIONS

This is an ideal way to help a youngster learn the number combinations that equal 10. For children who do not know them at the outset, I write down all the possible combinations so they can have them in front of them while they practice the trick. After several rehearsals most children discover that they can do without the cue cards.

Equipment. A deck of 52 cards.

Trick. Magician asks someone in the audience to pick a card from the pack, look at it and hold it. The magician quickly deals out the deck in rows, covering some of the cards to create piles. Then he picks up all of the piles, and names the card (denomination only) that is being held.

Magician's secret. As the cards are being dealt out, cover any pair of 10s, Jacks, Queens, or Kings. Cover any two cards that total 10. (Aces count as 1.) For example you would cover a 7 and a 3; and a 4 and a 6; two 5s, etc. When all of the cards have been dealt out, pick up any two piles that you would normally cover. Continue to remove the

piles—two at a time—until there is only one left. If the top card is a 10, Jack, Queen, or King, the hidden card is a 10, Jack, Queen or King respectively. Otherwise subtract the face value of the top card from 10 to determine the denomination of the card that has been taken from the deck. For example, if the top card on the remaining pile is a 7, the card held by the spectator is a 3 (10 − 7 = 3).

PENNY, NICKEL & DIME

I include this trick with some reservations. It is a little hard to learn and demands patience from both teacher and child who wants to perform it. But its effect is stunning, and the mastery of it makes it worthwhile for the young performer to stretch his memory, practice computation, and enhance his ability to analyze the sequence of sounds in words. It was for this last skill that I persisted and modified a more difficult trick into a form that most children (age nine and up) can cope with.

Performing the trick depends on the ability to memorize six key words and phrases in sequence, a very hard task for some youngsters. Children with learning disabilities usually find it a tremendous chore to learn arbitrary sequences of words or letters by rote. (This is why remembering the days of the week, and the months of the year gives them so much trouble.) Yet these same children can repeat long *meaningful* sentences, and learn words of songs or poems. It seemed important in adapting the trick to find key words that would make some kind of syntactic sense. Even if they were nonsense, if they could be read like English sentences, and repeated with normal intonation, it would facilitate memorizing.

Equipment. A penny, a nickel, a dime; and any 24 playing cards.

Trick. Magician puts a penny, a nickel and a dime on the table. He asks for three volunteers from his audience. He turns his back and each of the volunteers picks up a coin and puts it in his pocket. The magician then turns around, and deals out the cards—one to the first volunteer, two to the second, and three to the third. He leaves the remaining cards on the table. Then he turns his back again, and instructs the volunteers as follows: "If you have the penny, take as many cards as I gave you."

"If you have the nickel, take twice as many cards as I gave you."

"If you have the dime, take four times as many cards as I gave you."

The magician then turns around, picks up the remaining cards, and at once names the coin each volunteer is holding.

Magician's secret. The magician has memorized some nonsense sentences—one made up of three words: Panda Nipped Pudding; one made up of three parts that hang together: Stand up, Dopey Nut; Drink up!

After he has learned them he visualizes the separate parts as members of a list.

1. PaNDa
2. NiPpeD
3. PuDdiNg

5. staNDuP
6. DoPey Nut
7. DriNk uP

The list is numbered 1, 2, 3, 5, 6, 7. *There is no 4.*

The numbers represent the number of cards left on the table. The key words contain the order of the coins, with P = penny; N = nickel; and D = dime.

Thus if there is one card left over the magician visualizes his list: 1 = PaNDa. The order of the important letters in PaNDa is PND. Therefore the first volunteer has the penny; the second one has the nickel, and the third one has the dime.

If there are 6 cards left over, he thinks of item 6 in his list: DoPey Nut. He analyzes the sequence of sounds—comes up with DPN—representing the order of the coins. So the first volunteer has the dime, the second has the penny, and the third has the nickel.

ANIMAL, VEGETABLE, MINERAL

This is a mystifying mind-reading trick. The baffled audience will demand many repetitions certain that they can discover the magician's secret. No one ever does.

Learning Skills

Planning it and performing it:

• develops the ability to categorize • encourages children to talk and to listen • introduces the idea of mapping

---

Equipment. Any nine cards from a deck.

Trick. While the magician is out of the room, a member of the audience deals out nine cards in three rows of three. The audience chooses one of the cards without removing it. When the magician returns, the confederate, without even glancing at the cards, says one or two sentences; and the magician immediately points out the card. The trick can be repeated many times; the cards can be changed or rearranged; the confederate never says the same sentence twice, but the magician always chooses the right card.

Magician's secret. The magician and his confederate have agreed in advance that each of the cards stands for a category. The first horizontal row is designated Animal, Vegetable, Mineral. The second row is Man, Woman, Child; the third row is Color, Shape, Size. The confederate's sentence—seemingly irrelevant to the audience—contains a key word that signals the category, and therefore position of the card.

Thus, if the second card in the second row has been chosen by the audience, the confederate thinks: Woman; and might say, on the magician's return, "By the way, how's your Mother?"; or "Isn't it a shame about Marie Antoinette?"; or "Ladies first."

If, on the magician's return, the confederate said, "Raw carrots are better than cooked ones," the magician would think, "Vegetable," and remembering that the first row stands for Animal, Vegetable, Mineral, would point to the second card in the top row.

Before performing this trick in public, would-be magicians should practice by making sure they can correctly indicate the cards coded by the following sentences.

1. They have discovered gold in Alaska.
2. There's a new baby living next door to us.
3. Circles are nicer than squares.
4. There's a fly in the soup!
5. My sister is hungry.
6. What time does the milk man come?
7. That's a beautiful shade of red.
8. The fruit trees are in bloom.
9. What a big one!

Answers:

1. Third card, first row.
2. Third card, second row.
3. Second card, third row.
4. First card, first row.
5. Second card, second row.
6. Second card, second row.
7. First card, third row.
8. Second card, first row.
9. Third card, third row.

PAST, PRESENT, FUTURE

This is a variation on the previous trick, originally invented by my children and me to help my youngest son learn French verbs. Having had no training in grammar he found it hard to become aware of the way the tense of a verb was used to convey time reference. We did this many times first, in English. Then, when he had the idea, we did it in French.

Learning Skills

● develops awareness of time reference in sentences and the grammatical devices for expressing it (in English or any other language the child is studying)

● develops awareness of 1st, 2nd and 3rd person—especially useful in second language learning.

● encourages children to talk and to listen with care

● gives practice in mapping, using coordinates

The equipment and the trick are the same as in the preceding trick "Animal, Vegetable, Mineral." The magician's secret is different, though.

Magician's secret. The magician and his confederate have agreed in advance that the horizontal rows represent past, present and future respectively. The vertical columns represent 1st person, 2nd person and 3rd person respectively. To indicate the position of the card, the confederate determines the intersection of row and column and says an appropriate sentence.

If the audience has agreed on the first card in the first row, the confederate thinks "Past and First Person" and says something like "I went to the movies yesterday."

If the audience has agreed on the second card (2nd person) in the third row (future) the confederate might say, "Are you wearing your blue jeans tomorrow?"

If the magician hears "My brother has a bicycle," he thinks third person, present, and indicates the third card in the first row.

Would-be performers of this trick should practice locating the card indicated by the following clues.

1. The cat had kittens.
2. What time did you get up this morning?
3. I want a glass of water.
4. My neighbors are going on a trip next summer.

Answers: 1. Third card, first row.
2. Second card, first row.
3. First card, second row.
4. Third card, third row.

DIVERSIONS

Here are a number of card activities that do not qualify as games or card tricks, but *do* provide entertainment along with an intellectual challenge. I have used them as homework assignments. Teachers can use any of these as an activity for several children together, or an exercise for the entire class. The directions could be written on cards, and a card could be assigned to a child who had finished his more traditional work and was ready to move on to something new.

WHAT'S MY RULE?

With a deck of cards a teacher (or parent) can create a series of exercises to help develop inductive reasoning. Many psychologists believe that it is this kind of reasoning that underlies our ability to learn our native language and that it is this kind of reasoning that is involved in scientific theory construction.

In psychologists' experiments designed to investigate concept-formation, the experimenter devises a concept and his subject, shown positive and negative instances of it, tries to induce the rule or the conditions that must be fulfilled for membership in the secret class.

In the What's My Rule? exercises, the teacher pre-arranges the cards in a deck in accordance with a rule: The child is given the pack face-down, turns over the top card, and tries to predict what the next card will be. He may leave the cards he has turned over face up. He keeps track of the

number of correct predictions and continues to predict and turn over cards, one at a time, until he has discovered the rule which governed the arrangement of the cards and all his predictions are correct.

Several children may be given identical prepared decks and can compete to see who will have the greatest number of correct predictions; or who will be able to state the correct rule first.

Children may want to devise their own rules and create arrangements for each other.

Teachers can use a reduced deck and can ask children to predict only the color, or only the denomination of the cards in a pack, depending on the age and abilities of the child or how complicated they want to make the induction task.

Some sample arrangements and rules of varying difficulty follow:

Problem. Predict whether the next card will be red or black.

Arrangement.
1. Alternate the colors.
2. Two reds, two blacks, two reds, two blacks, etc.
3. Remove some of the reds and arrange the remaining

cards two black, one red, two black, one red, etc.

4. Omit face cards. Arrange the cards from 1 to 10 four times, so that in the first sequence odd numbers are black and even numbers are red, in the second sequence

odd numbers are red, and even numbers are black. In the third sequence even numbers red, and odd numbers black, and so on.

Problem. Predict the suit and denomination of the next card.

Arrangement.
1. For very young children use only one suit and arrange the cards in order from Ace to King.
2. Arrange the cards in order from King to Ace.
3. Arrange the cards so that all the Aces are on top, then the 2s, then the 3s, and so on up to Kings, with each foursome in the order spades, hearts, clubs, diamonds.
4. Omit the face cards. Arrange the cards in order 2, 4, 6, 8, 10 of spades, then Ace, 3, 6, 9 of hearts, then 2, 4, 6, 8, 10 of hearts, then Ace, 3, 6, 9 of clubs, then 2, 4, 6, 8, 10 of clubs, then Ace, 3, 6, 9 of diamonds, then 2, 4, 6, 8, 10 of diamonds, then Ace, 3, 6, 9 of spades.

Problem. Predict the suit and denomination of the next card.

Rule. A diamond is followed by a heart one higher in denomination.
A heart is followed by a spade one lower in denomination.
A spade is followed by a club one higher in denomination.
A club is followed by a diamond of the same denomination.
If the first card in the pre-arranged deck is the Ace of diamonds, then the Ace of hearts, King of spades and Ace of clubs will be omitted.

WHAT COMES NEXT?

Remembering items in a series and their order is an important ability for all children and a difficult task for many children with learning disabilities. This ability that underlies reading and spelling, learning verbal sequences like days of the week or months of the year can be practiced in a series of diversions systematically graded in difficulty.

Task. Child takes some cards off the top of the deck, looks at each one in turn and lays them face down in a row in front of him from left to right in the order in which he picked them up. He then turns them up one at a time, first trying to name in advance the card he is about to turn over. As soon as he faces up the card he knows whether or not his prediction was correct.

The task can be changed in difficulty:
1. By varying the number of cards—using 2, 3, 4 or 5.
2. By varying the requirements of what is recalled,
   e.g. color only
     denomination only
     suit only
     suit and denomination
3. By predicting the order of cards turned up one at a time from right to left, instead of left to right.
4. By decreasing the time in which they can look at each card.

In the easiest version, for children with very poor visual and verbal recall, three cards are chosen in advance, say three Queens, two red and one black. In this version, the child does not have to memorize the items, only their order. The cards are mixed, put in a pile face down. The child picks up the top card, says its color, and lays it face down at his left; picks up the next card, says it color and lays it face down to the right of the first one; picks up the third card, says its color and lays it face down at the end of the row. Then he faces the cards up in order from left to right each time naming the color of the card before he turns it over.

When he has mastered this with three, and then four cards, he can change the order in which he picks them up, working from right to left. At this point, he is developing his concepts of forwards and backwards, both in space and time.

Children with very poor immediate memory for what they see can be taught to rehearse the items verbally—mentally or aloud—to help them hang on to the series to be recalled. As a child's ability to remember improves, the difficulty of the memory task can be gradually increased. Keeping track of his progress adds to the child's interest in this diversion.

MAGIC SQUARE

Equipment. Nine cards: Ace, 2, 3, 4, 5, 6, 7, 8, 9—of any suit.

Problem. Arrange the cards in three rows of three cards each so that their face values total 15 in each row—horizontally, vertically and diagonally.

Solution.

6	7	2
1	5	9
8	3	4

CHALLENGE FOR TWO

Equipment. Thirteen cards: Ace through King, in any suit.

First of all. Lay out the cards face up in a row in sequence from Ace to King. Players take turns in picking up, in order, either one or two cards, starting with Ace.

The object of the game. To avoid having to pick up the king.

Challenge. To figure out how to win every time.

Solution. Let your opponent go first, and then make sure on your turn you take (and stop at) three, then six, then nine.

Variation. This time the object is to pick up the King.

Challenge. Is there a way to guarantee winning every time?

INDEX